D0483155

GOOD COMPANY

Julietta Dexter founded The Communications Store in 1995 with £600 and two clients. TCS would go onto become the premier strategic brand development, communications and PR company for some of the world's best brands in fashion, beauty and lifestyle, with offices in London and New York. In 2017 it was named as one of the *Sunday Times* Top 100 Small Companies to Work For. In 2020, The Communications Store became ScienceMagic.Inc.

GOOD COMPANY

HOW TO BUILD A BUSINESS
WITHOUT LOSING YOUR VALUES

JULIETTA DEXTER

Atlantic Books
London

First published in hardback and trade paperback in Great Britain in 2020
by Atlantic Books, an imprint of Atlantic Books Ltd.

This paperback edition published in 2021.

Copyright © Julietta Dexter, 2020

The moral right of Julietta Dexter to be identified as the author of this
work has been asserted by her in accordance with the Copyright, Designs
and Patents Act of 1988.

All rights reserved. No part of this publication may be reproduced, stored in
a retrieval system, or transmitted in any form or by any means, electronic,
mechanical, photocopying, recording, or otherwise, without the prior
permission of both the copyright owner and the above publisher of this book.

Every effort has been made to trace or contact all copyright holders. The
publishers will be pleased to make good any omissions or rectify any mistakes
brought to their attention at the earliest opportunity.

10 9 8 7 6 5 4 3 2

A CIP catalogue record for this book is available from the British Library.

Paperback ISBN: 978 1 78649 722 2
E-book ISBN: 978 1 78649 721 5

Printed in Great Britain

Atlantic Books
An imprint of Atlantic Books Ltd
Ormond House
26–27 Boswell Street
London
WC1N 3JZ

www.atlantic-books.co.uk

Contents

For my father,
John Dartnall Dexter CBE

Preface to the Paperback Edition

Good Company was originally published at the height of the first Covid-19 lockdown in the UK. Initially, it was difficult to know if this was good or bad timing. Perhaps people would be reading more at home. Perhaps people would be too preoccupied with the chilling medical realities of the pandemic to think about anything else. Perhaps business leaders would be too busy working out how to approach the many uncertainties their firms faced.

What a difference a year makes. With hindsight, I believe that Good Company was the right book for the moment. Yes, we have felt anxious, frightened, and unsure – unable to plan for the next week, let alone our futures. But a period of crisis is an excellent opportunity for evaluation. If one is lucky enough to have one's health, then one has a personal duty to protect others as best one can, and to use a moment like this, to listen, learn and search for improvement and self-awareness. This is especially true for anyone with responsibilities for others' careers and wellbeing. It's been immensely challenging.

Businesses, including The Communications Store (TCS), have had to make tough decisions. At times during 2020 we lost up to 35% of our revenue. Some of the brands we represented quite simply haven't made it – they could not 'pivot', to use a much overused word, quickly enough. It's been hideous. As a business leader, in a situation like this, you need to save as many jobs as you can. We've done all we can – no doubt making mistakes along the way – and we have lost exceptional talent, but we've sought to treat one another in the most respectful, dignified way possible. Putting people first.

On Friday 13 March 2020, we tested a day of remote working prior to the UK Government putting the country into lockdown. As I write this almost a year later, we're still not back in the office. Our work environment has evolved at an unprecedented pace and it is increasingly clear that the positive, and less positive, consequences of our new digital tools continue to need analysis, consideration and legal questioning. We've all embraced remote working by necessity and we're only just beginning to understand the longer-term implications, but, however we communicate, it is strong relationships and values that bind institutions and companies together.

In the middle of the Covid-19 crisis, another crisis exploded. The Black Lives Matter (BLM) movement erupted across the world, fuelled by footage of the killing of George Floyd in Minneapolis that shocked and horrified an already broken world. The movement opened our eyes to ongoing injustice, racism and inequality. It was another huge moment to pause, listen and learn. The swift and performative responses of many irked. But the truth is, this is going to take a long, long time to fix. In the past, the fact that we'd built a business that was 88% female was a statement of equality in itself. Not so anymore. Real diversity in the workplace has taken on a whole new meaning.

As a business, we were fortunate to already have an Inclusivity Committee, a group of people with minority lived experiences who had created a safe space to share, challenge and envision a better future. When the BLM movement rose up again, this committee set to work slowly, thoughtfully and with the mantra of not wanting to rush, but to create a plan that would last for years to come. We did make a donation to BLM but that was just a start. We must truly understand the inclusion of every single person and we must champion the power of real diversity. We have also just been accredited as B Corp and we are excited to join a community of like-minded businesses.

For many industries, but especially public relations and business development, 2020 felt like the end of an era. Consumer behaviour and the media landscape have changed more in the past year than in the past few decades. I was already concerned about these trends before the pandemic hit. We'd assembled a global advisory board in the Autumn of 2019 to interrogate the future of our business. How long could it continue as it was? As print media continued to dwindle and consumers spent ever more time on their mobile phones, I felt we needed to question our business model. Our global advisors had world-leading knowledge in tech, data science, the future of conscious consumerism, and the future of media. We gathered in our West London offices on 9 December 2019. When I left that meeting, I knew that it was time to rethink our business for new challenges.

And that's exactly what we've done. Never waste a crisis, they say. We've taken this time to shore up our existing business and be truthful about the parts that weren't working, that weren't innovative enough. And then we built a business model that brings together the best approach to using digital tools, data-driven power and an understanding of where the consumer will enjoy consuming (responsibly) in the future. On 18 October 2020 The Communications Store became ScienceMagic.Inc. It's a brave thing to do, and it certainly feels like a new beginning. TCS has been an independent company that has thrived for 25 years. It has been built on exceptional talent, hard graft, and shared values and business ethics – culture over strategy every, single, time. But we are evolving our talent to include different skills. I've partnered not only with Daniel, my existing business partner of 18 years, but also David Pemsel who was Chief Executive of the Guardian Media Group. He led the digital transformation of one of our most purpose-driven newspapers and brought it back to break-even after huge losses. He understands responsible digital transformation. It is a very exciting new chapter, but our values will remain at the centre of all we do.

What won't change is the core belief that business should be a force for good. Our ethics, our culture, and our values are paramount. We will remain a company where profit alone is not the only goal. And we will continue to strive for a world where businesses are more transparent, more open, more communicative, and greater contributors to wider society. I've learnt so much this far, but I am committed to a life of learning. There's never just one way to do things. I want to keep challenging myself, learning new things, from new people around me.

In 1995 when I spoke of kindness, values and ethics in the workplace, many patronised and belittled me. Focus on your bottom line to be successful, they said. But today we live in a world where organisations can no longer ignore their environmental, social and wider economic impact. Such discussions should be at the top of the agenda in C-suite meetings. This is why I've taken the role of Chief Growth & Purpose Officer at ScienceMagic.Inc. so I can focus on what really matters. I hope this book reveals why doing so is the best avenue to long-term success.

Julietta Dexter
January 2021

Introduction
The Future Is Friendly

I've always been interested in business. I remember being very small, less than ten years old, and watching my father, the owner of an insurance company, come home with his briefcase and put his papers down on his desk; words, numbers, calculations, letters, documents and neat, meticulous, to-do lists. My father was always getting things done. He would read the newspaper in the evenings in the sitting room. I always thought it looked clever and was such a good use of time, finding out what was going on in the world, what was happening in the business community. I wanted to be like him and make intelligent use of my time, too.

My father died quite shockingly in 1991 at the age of fifty-eight while I was in my final year at the University of Cambridge. He went to sleep one night and just didn't wake up in the morning. At his funeral, hundreds of people showed up to pay their respects – not only friends, family and neighbours, but all of his eighty or so employees, lots of people he'd met through his business and all the other extraordinary things he did outside of work, too. He contributed a lot. It was humbling to see just how many lives he'd touched in his lifetime. I am now fifty and have had more years without my father than with him. But losing him so suddenly was a personal trauma that has shaped my life, my behaviour and my thinking every day, as both a human being and as a business person.

In the year after his death, I watched my friends from university go into banking, management consultancy and graduate trainee programmes with law firms and accountancy practices – Oxbridge cream-of-the-crop graduates for tomorrow's job market. My route into the job market wasn't quite such a straight line. First, I went back to our family's home in Italy to help my mother with my late father's affairs. Then I returned to London, applied for endless jobs and received forty rejections. I was pretty low and lost, to be honest.

A family friend, Charlotte de Vita (who went on to be hugely successful in the charitable field), helped me land my first job at The English-Speaking Union, a philanthropic organization that fostered good relationships between the UK and the US in the fields of art, literature, music and education, and where I had the privilege of working with a small group of great, hard-working people. From the charity sector, I went into the world of fashion and beauty communications. Those two worlds – charity and PR – could not have been more different. One was well-meaning, humble and under-funded. The other was insincere, vainglorious and under-handed. My early jobs as an account associate taught me everything I needed to know about how *not* to run a business.

I lasted a few years at what was, to me, a miserable office until I quit in protest when my boss instructed me to increase our clients' fees by 30 per cent for no reason at all. Unemployed and with no idea what to do next, I got a call from a former client who wanted to know why I'd left my previous job. I shared the story and confided to him that I liked being an accounts person in the communications field, but the corporate culture I'd seen so far had left me demoralized. Maybe I was naïve, but I'd worked hard throughout my education and did my honest best for a boss who tore down my confidence on a daily basis. Was this really all the job market had to offer? Was this what I'd worked so hard for?

The ex-client said, 'Start your own business and do it your way.'

My initial reaction was to laugh. I was only twenty-five and lacked the skills and experience to start my own company. When I was a girl, my father would sometimes joke about me taking over his business someday, but I thought that was more fatherly flattery than a serious possibility. And yet, I was intrigued by the idea nonetheless, certainly enough to talk about it over dinner with that client and my then-husband. Both men were supportive and encouraging. They believed in me and felt I could actually make a go of it. So, the next day, I started jotting down some thoughts which ultimately turned into a business plan.

In retrospect, it was all a bit rash. I didn't have a lot else going on then, so there was no harm in scribbling down ideas. Doing my on-paper conceptualizing, I see now, was a brave act. A lot of dreamers with great ideas don't get that far. They just flow from one notion to the next, one dissatisfying job to the next, and never write down what they'd do on their own if they could. Fear and self-doubt are the biggest roadblocks to success. Writing a one-page, broad-strokes description of a future company is not like signing a legal contract. It's little more than doodling on a cocktail napkin. But unless someone takes that step, they'll never move forward.

Oh, I had plenty of doubts. Even as I worked on my plan, I kept asking myself, 'Can I *really* start a business?' and had to stop myself from crumpling my papers into a ball and throwing them over my shoulder. What kept me going was a hunger to prove myself and defy the industry standard by founding a company that would and could break the mould of the old-fashioned business model I'd seen so far, defined by short-term profit-taking, bosses who ruled by fear and intimidation, hierarchies that turned colleagues against each other and an aggressive 'winner-takes-all' approach that encouraged unhappy workplaces. In my future company, I'd change all of that, and create a safe place to take risks, with compassion guiding all aspects of the business. A part of my character works on 'competitive rebellion' (according to my business coach). Proving to myself that I could do things differently was the motivation that kept me going.

During this uncertain time, I felt my father's absence keenly. It'd been several years since he'd died, and I wished he could give me guidance and weigh in on countless issues that came up. My plan from the start was to mirror his 'no-bullshit' style of doing business. Memories of how he ran his company were my main inspiration. While clearing out his home office, my sisters and I found drawers and boxes full of my father's paperwork. He wrote multiple drafts of letters, beautifully handwritten, with courtesy and gratitude on every page. He had been a careful, considered and considerate man in all of his correspondences, a far cry from how we communicate now. (I wonder what he would make of Twitter attacks and Facebook trolling. In fact, I wonder a lot about how he would handle just about everything related to business today.) My father closed his office every Friday at lunchtime, not just during the summer, but year-round, so his staff was free to see the dentist, have a kid's birthday party, get an early start on a weekend trip or keep a plumber's appointment. According to a document I discovered in a drawer, he gave options to eight of his employees so that they could share in the sale profits, too. He didn't have to, but he did. He'd made plenty of money while taking good care of his people and had a great life while staying true to his values.

From what I'd experienced so far, these qualities seemed to be outside the corporate norm at the time. The stressed-out, anxious people I'd met from other agencies in the same field had similar complaints. Instead of being guided or nurtured by their managers, they were often patronized and belittled. The business model for PR – and most other industries – appeared to be to 'get as much as you can and give the very least' on every front, from the unfair and unkind treatment by bosses, to the deliverables for journalists and clients. At least in one of my previous jobs, my colleagues and I were all very much united in loathing our boss and in support of each other. But at most bullshit offices, there's an 'everyone for himself' mindset, making them a well-dressed version of *The Hunger Games*.

As I understood it then, making money was a traditional business model's justification for unethical behaviours – cooking the books, overcharging clients, underpaying staff. The companies where I'd seen such practices *were* profitable and successful. I had to wonder whether it was even possible to build a human-friendly company and also make money. Were honesty, kindness and compassion profitable commodities? My father had done it, but was he an anomaly or a throwback? Was his wise alternative to short-termism no longer possible in the mid-1990s business world? I was resolved to try to live my life and operate my business with his old-school morals nonetheless, and to just see what happened.

I initially wanted to incorporate my new company as 'NO. BS. PR' but eventually chose a name that was a bit less confrontational but no less transparent. I called it The Communications Store (TCS). My one-woman operation launched in 1995 from a windowless shared office. I didn't have a lot going for me – just youthful enthusiasm, £600 in seed money, two clients and a vision of what a compassionate business could be. One phone call at a time, I built my reputation as being steady and honest, a far cry from the 'Fabulous, darling!' *Ab Fab* fashion PR stereotype of saying everything and doing nothing.

In 1996, I brought in a former colleague from my *Devil Wears Prada* days to become my first partner. Tom Konig-Oppenheimer and I worked together to build TCS, and the company grew quickly. In 2002, we were joined by Daniel Marks, still my business partner today. Before long, we had a team of five, then fifteen, all the way up to our current 200 employees in London and New York. Our client roster increased from two to five, ultimately to scores of the world's top luxury brands. Some of our clients, in no particular order, have included Versace, Glossier, MaxMara, Molton Brown, Moët & Chandon, Diptyque, Ferragamo, Chantecaille, Orlebar Brown, Rocco Forte Hotels,

Christopher Kane, House of Holland, NET-A-PORTER, Allbirds, BaByliss, Burberry Beauty, ESPA, John Frieda and Rolls-Royce. Our annual billing is in the tens of millions of pounds.

Along with attracting and retaining this calibre of client, we've been recognized within our industry with numerous awards and honours and have become known as one of the top strategic brand development, PR and communications companies in the fashion, lifestyle and beauty arena. We help brands communicate, grow and, above all, be aspirational and desirable to consumers the world over. In 2019, we were named the number one fashion, beauty and luxury communications agency by *PRWeek UK*. In 2018, we made the list in the *Sunday Times* 100 Best Small Companies, based on our employee feedback score in eight key areas: leadership, management, engagement, personal growth, peer relationships, well-being, salaries and social responsibility – confirmation that we are achieving our goal of doing well by being good to each other.

We've established a successful, widely admired company by upholding compassionate principles that have long been unheard of in business. By being unwilling to compromise on our 'no-BS' culture, we've thrived in every sense of the word. Of all our accomplishments, I feel most strongly about the longevity of our relationships with many of our staff and our clients, some of whom have been with us since the beginning. We've stuck to our promises and principles, and they've stuck with us. They wouldn't have stayed with us, for decades in some cases, if we hadn't made plenty of money for them – this is a business after all – but also if we hadn't stuck to our human-friendly values.

I don't want to give you the impression that the road from that windowless shared office to our present locations at the WestWorks campus in White City, London, and Spring Street in Manhattan's Soho neighbourhood was strewn with rose petals (although it was often slathered with Dr. Hauschka's Rose Day Cream). We've had lean and really tough years. I've faltered, made big mistakes, made an idiot of myself and doubted myself all along the way. But during the down cycles, no matter how bleak our prospects, we were motivated by our strong relationships. We cared about each other too much to fail. When you put people first, you learn exactly how determined and resilient you can be.

I know talking about caring and feelings isn't something a stereotypical CEO would do. I wonder if forced-to-resign former WPP CEO Martin Sorrell comforts himself during his dark nights of the soul by reflecting on how well he's treated others. Is being ruthless the answer? Maybe for some, but it's just not for me. When people ask me what skills I bring to work as a leader, I often say my 'maternal' skills; encouragement and support, patience and nurturing. At home – with my daughters and my (second and, God help me, last) husband – we practise care, respect and consideration. My colleagues, staff and clients are my work family, and we treat each other the same way. It's our company policy to take care of each other.

I'd rather make less money than hurt or use anyone. In fact, we sometimes *have* made a little less by choice so that we wouldn't have to work with brands that were in conflict with our core values. We ask ourselves if we believe in the people behind the product and the product itself. If we don't, we don't work with them. Perhaps, in the short-term, we would have a bigger bank balance if we'd taken on certain dubious clients. But it would have been a bad 'return on ethics' in the long-term, reflecting negatively on us and damaging our reputation. Besides that, I wouldn't have been able to sleep at night.

Looking back at all the relationships we've built, at employees I've hired for their first jobs and seen grow up, at the clients and small brands we've grown into global stars, I know that I've done well by my father's memory and stayed true to his inspiration. With the hard work of my brilliant partners – Tom for nineteen years and then fashion business legend Daniel Marks – and our entire international team, we've built a company I hope my father would be proud of.

It's been twenty-five years since I founded TCS. But in many ways, times haven't changed. BS corporate culture is still very much in place. You see evidence of it in pay gaps and income inequality. Maximizing short-term returns to shareholders and making money matters more than improving the quality of life for the majority of a company's workers. The financial crisis in 2008 was a perfect example of the smash-and-grab tactics that made some bankers rich in the short-term and proved catastrophically ineffective in the long-term, ruining lives and wiping out the savings of millions. Although the global economy has recovered, corporate greed and mistreatment of staffers by tyrannical bosses continue to be front-page news.

Even the biggest, seemingly impervious leaders and companies are being held accountable for their bad behaviour and lack of ethics. In 2018, *The New York Times* and *The Observer* exposed the machinations of British political consultancy

Cambridge Analytica's duplicity in acquiring private data from Facebook users and exploiting that information to influence the 2016 US presidential election and many others. The British government issued a warrant to investigate the firm's crimes, and Cambridge Analytica has since closed operations.[1] An affiliate tech firm, Canada's AggregateIQ, went through a similar comeuppance when a whistle-blower revealed its role in manipulating voters in making their Brexit decision. As a result, AggregateIQ was suspended from Facebook and served a notice by the UK Information Commissioner's Office for breaking European privacy laws. And look at Sir Philip Green, the former chairman of the retail company Arcadia Group (whose brands include Topshop, Topman and Miss Selfridge). He once owned the home retailer BHS, a brand that lost 11,000 jobs, owed £1.2 billion and ran a pension deficit of £571 million when it went out of business. Meanwhile, Green and his family collected £586 million during his fifteen years of mismanaging the retailer.[2] Winner takes all, regardless of the consequences. In 2019, Green's reputation took another blow when *The Telegraph* reported on his racist, sexist misbehaviour at Arcadia. At the time of writing, his empire is near collapse.[3]

All of these and so many more offensive examples of BS business only make a stronger case for the emergence of companies with the long-term, relationship-based values that have traditionally been seen as soft and feminine, but are anything but. We need more companies to shift towards a no-BS culture of compassion. Given the divisive political climate of late, we could all use more fairness, kindness and collaboration in our lives. There is as much uncertainty now, thanks to Brexit, as there was during the Great Recession. No one knows what the landscape of business is going to look like over the next decade. Being inclusive and kind as a strategy for forging new partnerships seems like a smart idea.

The public learned from the recession to no longer tolerate corporate tricks. Unethical companies and CEOs are being found out and held accountable. According to a report on CEO succession at 2500 of the world's largest companies, top bosses in the UK are removed, on average, after just 4.8 years, due in part to public and shareholder scrutiny and criticism of unethical behaviours such as fraud, sexual harassment and mismanagement, down from 8.3 years in 2010.[4] What's more, at the largest of those companies, the CEO is almost twice as likely to be forced out due to ethical lapses.

People are clueing in to the fact that lack of compassion in the workplace isn't sustainable. Workplace stress, aka burnout, is at epic proportions. According to a 2018 study by the UK government's Health and Safety Executive, 595,000 British workers suffer anxiety and depression related to their work; British employers lost 15.4 million working days due to employee stress during the study period.[5] Stress stats are climbing year on year. A study by the American Psychological Association found that the US economy loses $500 billion due to workplace stress every year, with 550 million missed workdays.[6] Stress caused between 60 and 80 per cent of all workplace accidents.

Workaholism undermines bosses as well. In 2018, Tesla founder Elon Musk's workaholic lifestyle was exposed in a *New York Times* article, describing a tumultuous year in his business.[7] He worked 120 hours per week, never took time off, used AMBIEN to sleep if he slept at all (sometimes under his desk at the office) and had no time for his kids or anything but work, all to satisfy the unyielding demands of 'short-seller' shareholders. A month after that article appeared, he was forced to resign as chairman of the company's board. That same year, as further evidence of his unravelling, Musk had a front-page spat with the brave men and women trying to rescue a team of trapped young footballers in a cave in Thailand, calling one of his critics a paedophile. His ego and ambition seemed to come before all else: his family, his friends, and his physical and emotional health.

Trying the opposite of BS profit-over-people – putting people first – is actually profitable in and of itself. According to a 2017 report in *Forbes* magazine, the 'Just 100' – the 100 most fair and ethically responsible companies in the US – generated, on average, a 3.5 per cent higher 5-year return on invested capital, paid employees better, had more female board members, created more jobs, paid eight times fewer corporate fines and donated twice as much to charity than their off-the-list competitors.[8] According to a 2017 McKinsey study, a company is more likely to be successful if its culture is ethical, empathetic and diverse in terms of gender, ethnicity, ability and age.[9] Employees who work for a friendly, forward-thinking organization are more likely to excel at their job, and less likely to develop cardiovascular disease later in life.[10] A healthy, happy – no-BS – workplace is essential to the well-being of a company's employees and to its profitability. In my humble opinion, you can't and shouldn't have one without the other.

For companies to attract new talent, they must be socially responsible in a local or global sense. By 2025, Millennials will make up 75 per cent of the global workforce.[11] According to a recent study of 1000 college-educated Americans born since 1981, 86 per cent enthusiastically agreed with the statement, 'Knowing I am helping to make a positive difference in the world is more important to me than professional recognition.'[12] Seventy-nine per cent concurred with the statement, 'My work environment will be more important than the paycheck.' Job seekers of my daughters' generation are just not interested in working insane hours in a cubicle to make their boss or the company's shareholders rich. They want to do fulfilling work that's positive for themselves and their communities. Traditional companies that put quarterly profits above all else should be worried. To attract the best, most creative young talent, they will need to change their big-picture objectives to be inspiring and benevolent. There has to be a positive vision.

It restores one's faith in our future to know that leaders of the next generation care more about social responsibility than grabbing what they can for themselves. My husband often says that the people who will be remembered long into the future will be those who make a positive impact, and I totally agree. Will the guy who worked all hours and made more money than anyone else at the expense of those around him be the one we laud and celebrate twenty, fifty or 100 years from now? Or will we honour those who changed the world for the better? It's the same for companies. I've already mentioned some companies with questionable ethics that have been undone by their scandals. To survive into the next decade, the winner-takes-all, uncaring, competitive, BS, stereotypically 'male' style can and should be replaced with an inclusive, caring, collaborative, no-BS, stereotypically 'female' one.

When you internalize and exhibit kindness and consideration at work, people return the favour. Some people call this 'paying it forward'. And, frankly, TCS's reputation for common decency has driven the business all along. The tone of any company starts at the top. It's up to leadership to uphold values and behaviours, and to spread the message to others in the industry, and beyond. Every time a person or a company behaves in an upstanding integral manner, it has a positive ripple effect. My main objective as CEO is bigger than promoting brands. I'm promoting transparency and compassion, in-house and with our clients' products, which are valued and appreciated by people all over the world. It's possible that one ethical office in the UK will inspire another and another, and soon creative and corporate workers will be happier and healthier everywhere. That's the big idea anyway: start small and expand compassionate culture around the world.

You can see the shift happening already, when a grossly unethical firm goes out of business, a CEO resigns in disgrace, a company is fined billions of dollars for wrongdoing (as Facebook was in April 2019 for privacy violations), or a female or ethnic minority worker ascends to a high-level job. It should certainly happen more often. There are too few leaders who really put their working community out front, and far too many who will prioritize short-term profit above the very people that make the work happen in the first place.

One of the main reasons I'm writing this book is to call attention to the need for positive change in the world of business, and to inspire leaders to drive that change and workers to rally for it. When thousands or millions of workers stand up and demand that their companies do more to improve the quality of life for employees, save the environment and balance inequalities, the company will benefit. But that's only the beginning. Although, to cynical ears, this might sound like BS (it's not), I truly believe that the good work of just one person can help people far and wide. Positive change has to start somewhere, so why not here and now? The 'how' is in this book.

To be honest, I struggled with climbing up on this soapbox, right from the outset. It's not natural for me to put myself forward. However, I have been leading a company that has succeeded in creating a friendly and compassionate corporate culture, and I have learned a lot over the last twenty-five years about how to do it. I have some wisdom to impart that might be of use to people who hope to start a no-BS business one day or foster a human-friendly change in the place they are currently working.

It all goes back to my long-ago decision to quit that job and start a company based on my father's principles. My life changed for the better when I fixated on that one tiny phrase – 'no BS' – as a guideline for how I wanted to live and lead. Anyone with dreams of a compassionate, ethical corporate future would do well to keep that phrase in mind, too. It's the central philosophy of this book, and my life.

On these pages, you'll discover stories, research, advice and ideals about no-BS values and leadership style. You'll also find stories and examples about the opposite – the toxic, BS culture that still dominates too much of the corporate world today. I want to be clear that friendly doesn't mean lazy. Ethical, compassionate people still need to work very hard. At TCS, it's not a winner-takes-all battlefield, but it's no walk in the park either. As long as you are ambitious and understand the rigorous demands of success, you can make it in business without lying, cheating or harming others. It's possible, and preferable, to fulfil your professional dreams in a softer, kinder manner. No BS allowed, no bloodshed required.

1 Leadership

Let's start with a tale of two bosses at two old American companies.

Eddie Lampert became the CEO, chairman and principle shareholder of 120-year-old Sears Holdings in 2005. At the time, the retail company had a dozen iconic brands (including Sears, Kmart, Land's End, Kenmore and BLACK+DECKER, among others) and 3500 stores nationwide. Although Sears got through the Great Depression in the 1930s, and both World Wars, it could not survive online shopping. Over Lampert's fourteen-year ownership of the company, it dwindled to just over 200 stores and declared bankruptcy in 2018. Critics blame Lampert's management. Instead of investing in the company, creating a competitive online platform and rebranding to attract a younger customer base, Lampert used capital to buy back shares in the company (inflating the per share price), and sold pieces of it for hundreds of millions of dollars. The sales benefited him, as the company's largest shareholder, and offset Sears's (and his) debt.

Lampert owns a real estate investment fund, Seritage Growth Properties, that Sears stores paid rent to, essentially paying millions to himself. Lampert will benefit again when the company's remaining assets are liquidated in a fire sale. Experts estimate that in all his machinations, Lampert stripped the company of $2 billion. In 2018, while top Sears executives petitioned for millions in bonuses, thousands of employees were losing their jobs, benefits or severance payments.[1] Due to mismanagement, greed and cultural change, a once great company was brought to its knees, and only the man at the very top will come out okay.

Another great, 100-year-old American company, the Campbell Soup Company, was led by Denise Morrison from 2011 to late 2018. In her seven years as CEO, she transformed the stodgy brand into one that focused on its customers' health and on social responsibility. She launched initiatives to fight hunger and childhood obesity; fostered a culture of volunteerism by having employees volunteer at soup kitchens to feed the poor; encouraged and supported women's rise in the ranks; and called for mandatory labelling of genetically modified organisms on all food product labels. She acquired other companies that would appeal to younger, health-conscious consumers, like the juice company Bolthouse Farms and organic baby food company Plum Organics. Morrison tried new marketing ideas that didn't always work – like selling soup in pouches – but, as she once said, 'The world of marketing has changed. You can lead the change or be a victim of change.'[2] Unfortunately, her tenure as boss ended in 2018 after a three-year stock slump. But during her last year at the helm, she was named by *Forbes* magazine as one of the world's most reputable CEOs.[3]

One leader grabbed as much as he could for himself while his company collapsed at his feet. The other tried to drive social change and engage both her employees and customers while experimenting to save the brand. Morrison landed safely and comfortably on the board of directors at Visa after her time at Campbell Soup ended. In April 2019, Lampert, still owner but no longer chairman of Sears, was sued by his own company which sought repayment of 'billions of dollars in value' that they claimed Sears had 'looted'.[4]

Lampert embodies the traditional, BS, stereotypically more 'male' leadership style of a winner-takes-all mentality that's driven by short-term gain. The BS boss is master, and everyone in the company is there to do their bidding and be at their service. It's all about taking everything for oneself at the expense of everyone else.

Morrison represents the kinder, responsible, no-BS alternative, an ideology called 'servant leadership'. A servant boss uses their position to benefit and engage the company's employees and customers in a long-term gain, a one-for-all-and-all-for-one egalitarian meritocracy of people working together towards a common purpose. In Morrison's case, she was driven by the purpose of bringing an old-fashioned brand into the present in its products, social environment and office culture. That's the no-BS brand of leadership I try to learn and practise, and continually aspire to.

Of course, this is not to say that every man has a 'male' leadership style or that every woman has a 'female' style. Every person, regardless of gender, probably has a mix of both aggression and passivity; of being motivated by competition or collaboration; of wanting to crush or help; and of looking for quick wins or long-term strategies.

The future of corporate success depends on leadership shifting in a nurturing, caring direction, of having a purpose larger than just one's own greed and ego. To be completely honest, I practise 'servant leadership' because it works. When you have a reputation for being a decent human being who cares about people and the world we live in, clients want to do business with you and employees want to work with you. They'll return the good vibes and behaviours to the benefit of all. You don't *command* respect, ever; you *earn* it slowly, carefully and over a long period of time.

A Bully Is Not an Effective Boss

As the saying goes, 'People don't quit jobs, they quit bosses.'

Bully bosses might believe that yelling and threatening is the best way to motivate employees, but according to research, being an abusive supervisor does not lead to greater employee productivity.[5] It makes no sense for a leader to rule by cruelty and fear. Why undermine and rattle the very people you need to get the job done?

There is a big discussion going on in brands and in business about the value of kindness. Traditional competitive-style leaders might think kindness is a kind of weakness, but it costs nothing and adds so much value to every interaction. Even when I have to do tough stuff, I have always tried to be kind.

A good leader practises kindness and patience to gently encourage workers to do their best work. I've used these same tools to defuse bullies who might've taken a look at me and decided I was an easy target. On one occasion, a client, the CEO of an apparel company, was trying to bully me into doing more work for less money, and he was relentless. It got to the point where I struggled not to show my frustration whenever I was in his presence. You know that feeling when you have a lump in your throat or you think you might cry, but bite it back because you've been told you should never show vulnerability? Bursting into tears in a meeting is not deemed to be professional. I got it in my head that if I cried in front of him, particularly as a female, I'd lose my dignity, my upper hand and reveal my weakness.

While struggling to stay in the discussion and not break down, I realized that I could never make my case in an emotional state. I had to separate myself from my immediate emotional reaction in order to find my wiser, more rational self.

The next time this client started to berate me, I said in a perfectly calm, quiet voice, 'Excuse me, I'm going to take myself out of this conversation. I don't accept or appreciate the way you're speaking to me, and I think I'm about to cry.' Then I got up and left the room. No drama, no emotion, just fact. The reprieve gave me a chance to collect myself before I went back in.

When I returned a few minutes later, he was chagrined and begged me to forgive him. Then he opened up about the pressures he was under and how he might have been trying to transfer some of that to me. Because I showed my *honest* vulnerability, he then showed me his stresses and strains. He felt horrible and wanted to know what he could do to make it up to me. Suddenly, he was the vulnerable person at the table. I'm not saying it was like magic... but, actually, it was. Truth and honesty prevailed. Once we'd both expressed ourselves, we could work together with a new understanding and trust.

Leaders are not impervious to emotion. They're not made of stone. A wise leader is brave enough to express their feelings to reclaim authority over them. To be human.

JUST WALK AWAY

If someone makes you feel small with aggression, they are trying to control you. If you state your feelings in a calm voice, and then physically remove yourself, you are not being controlled. And you are also not being unprofessional in any way at all. Distance gives you the space to rebuild boundaries around yourself. Whether it's a corridor, the loos or a step outside, just be alone for a moment – this energetically shuts down that negative interaction.

Take a moment to do a few rounds of deep breathing – inhale through your nose into your belly, hold it for a few seconds and then exhale through your mouth. This will help you to re-centre, allowing you to calm down and speak rationally.

And next time you are in a meeting that takes a bad turn, have the presence of mind to take your phone out, put it on the table, say 'Is it all right if I record this?' and press record. In the digital age of whistle-blowers, leaks and hacks, it's no longer possible for leaders to hide bad language, behaviour and practices in the shadows. I expect we'll see many, many more examples of worker revolts and bosses being called out by brave employees and toppled because of the untenable workplaces they have created.

Leaders Have to Lead

This story comes from a friend – a very successful journalist who started her career in public relations – about a bully boss who was also an incompetent manager:

It was my first day at a new job and no one told me what I was supposed to do. I was basically shown a desk, handed a bunch of files and told to have a go at it. If not for my sympathetic desk mate, I would have had no idea what to do. I was never given real direction, but still expected to do everything exactly as the boss wanted. He vacillated between micromanagement and neglect. One day, he'd hover over me when I was trying to write a press release, correcting me as I typed each word. The next, he was unavailable to give any kind of direction, and would then scream at me when I submitted my work because it wasn't what he wanted. From one day to the next, I'd be his favourite or his target, but I never understood what I'd done right or wrong as the case might be.

One time, I was unexpectedly called into a meeting with a new client. I had no time to prepare and didn't know a thing about the brand. The boss introduced me to the client and commanded me to start pitching on the spot. The whole thing was incredibly stressful, and I stammered my way through an incoherent, vague general pitch that made me sound like a fool. The boss told me to go back to my desk. When he found me later, he called me 'worthless' and 'an idiot' in front of my colleagues. I left that job soon after. It wasn't just the daily abuse and humiliation. I wasn't learning anything – except how to cringe whenever the boss came near my desk.

A no-BS leader is a guide who gives information and instruction to their staff so they have every opportunity to do well. As such, a good leader/guide provides each worker with guidelines. What is the job? What does it entail? What are the requirements? How can each person, to the best of their ability, get their job done well?

Part of our leadership at TCS is to set clearly defined, reachable benchmarks for each employee, on a daily or weekly basis, as well as a biannual to-do list. Every six months, we meet with each employee to go over whether they've hit their six-month objectives. If somebody clears their goals, pay reviews and promotions are reviewed annually, sometimes even every six months, particularly for newer, younger members. If they don't clear those goals, we know about it. (Really, there's nowhere to hide. In huge corporations, you can organize by committee and just muddle through. Our company isn't big enough for people to coast.)

Treat Everyone as an Equal

When I was eight years old, I remember walking through the cobbled street in tiny, rural Cardano, Italy (population about 800), an ancestral village where people had lived off the land for hundreds of years. Dad worked in Milan during the week and we went up to Cardano on Lake Como every weekend. One day, we ran into Dad's friend, Baron Pier Fausto Bagatti Valsecchi, a warm, calm man whose aristocracy somehow instinctively impressed. I asked him with the innocence of a kid, 'What's it like to be a Baron?' I didn't even know what that was.

He said, 'If you are a Baron, you get to treat every single person, whether they are a tramp or a King, in exactly the same way. That is your duty and privilege.'

I took the Baron's principle to heart and have since done my best to treat everyone I work with, be they the rich and famous or young staff, with the same respect and politeness. I've noticed that all really great leaders do this.

In 2007, I flew to Dublin for the day to meet with our client Bryan Meehan. Bryan is a serial entrepreneur, he owned Fresh & Wild market, sold it to Whole Foods, then founded skincare brand NUDE, with Ali Hewson, incredible wife of Bono, and then bought the Blue Bottle Coffee Company, to name just a few of his business interests.

In our meeting, we discussed how TCS could help publicize and market NUDE, and we all got along quite well. Towards the end of the meeting, we learned that a major storm was coming in, and unless I left immediately to catch an earlier flight back to London, I would be stuck overnight. We busily worked out what to do, and the plan was for me to go straight to the airport from the meeting. It seemed important to Bono to make sure I got home safely and on time for dinner with my kids. He insisted on carrying my suitcase himself quite a long way to the car. It was such a kind gesture. I was, frankly, beyond embarrassed. Ten other people could have been helped me, or I could have carried my own bag quite easily. But Bono wouldn't take no for an answer. So polite, so kind, he thanked me for my time and apologized about the change in schedule. I was absolutely floored by his graciousness.

Compare that story to this one. In 2010, I was very lucky to be invited to a reception of 100 top UK entrepreneurs at 10 Downing Street. Baroness Kate Rock coordinated the guest list and graciously thought to include me. She and I were among the few women at the reception itself. When I walked into the garden where the reception was held, I saw many, many suits and only a handful of dresses. The ratio was probably 1 to 10.

I'll be honest enough to admit that walking into the gardens of 10 Downing Street, one of the few women there, was nerve-wracking. I was by myself, scanning the crowd, really hoping I saw a familiar face to talk to so I wouldn't have to stand alone on the edge. I spotted a senior member of a PR firm, a man I'd met several times before. My face lit up, and I immediately went over to him to say hello. I smiled and said, 'Hi, how are you?' He barely looked at me and turned his back to talk to someone else, someone he quite clearly deemed more important than me.

It was a shaky start to what turned out to be a wonderful night. I met David Cameron, and we had a great little conversation. I chatted with some industry leaders outside of my field, which is always fascinating. It was a privilege to be there, and I never thought otherwise. My firm was small, of course, compared to some of the entrepreneurial giants in attendance. At that time, the man who blanked me had a huge firm, and he was quite powerful. Now, it no longer exists. But if I saw him at a party tomorrow, I wouldn't turn my back on him. That is just rude.

It doesn't matter how famous, important and amazing someone is, people should never lord so-called importance over others they perceive as beneath them. Very often, people who *think* they're at the top of the tree try to block anyone else from climbing up. But if they really are at the top, like Bono, they would lend a hand to help others get there.

Bono gets it. So does Vernon Hill. Vernon Hill and his wife Shirley sit at the top of the highest tree in the global business world. Vernon founded and chairs Metro Bank in the UK and Commerce Bancorp in the US. Vernon and Shirley, or should I say Mr and Mrs Hill, have been so generous to me over the years. Most recently, Vernon phoned my mobile directly to offer me an introduction to a piece of new business. That someone so successful is so accessible and generous with his time is quite surprising and beyond inspiring. No-BS leadership is not about measuring who's important enough to be worth talking to. It's more like, 'Let's talk! Let's work together!' I admire Shirley Hill enormously too − she always has time, and is so encouraging of and interested in TCS's business efforts and plans. They are both an example of real positive energy and leadership.

Never Abuse Power

The #MeToo Movement began in 2018 with a *New York Times* article that exposed movie producer Harvey Weinstein's abuse of actresses throughout his career. The UK has its very own Harvey Weinstein in the figure of Sir Philip Green, chairman of the Arcadia Group. According to a report first published by

The Daily Telegraph (only possible after an injunction to suppress the story was lifted), five women accused the businessman of groping, swatting bottoms, putting a female staffer in a headlock in front of others, calling a woman 'naughty girl', commenting on women's weight, kissing them in front of other staffers, and prodding, poking, grabbing and making them feel uncomfortable. When one unnamed accuser complained to HR about his behaviour, she was paid hundreds of thousands of pounds in exchange for her signing a non-disclosure agreement; another – the 'naughty girl' – was paid £1 million for her silence.

Green's lawyers denied the accusations, describing him as a 'Passionate businessman, who can at times be overexuberant and hot-headed... perceived at times as aggressive with senior and trusted staff.'[6]

The *Telegraph*'s editor, Chris Evans, saw the bigger picture and said, 'We are delighted the injunction has been lifted, but our campaign against the misuse of NDAs goes on. In the wake of the Harvey Weinstein affair, we became aware that gagging orders called NDAs were being used to cover up allegations of sexual misconduct and racial abuse in the workplace. And that led to our investigation into Sir Philip Green and Arcadia. We maintain there is a clear public interest in telling people whether a prospective employer has been accused of abuse.'[7]

The culture of harassment and abuse is coming to an end. We can only hope that stereotypical 'male' aggression, archcompetitiveness and ruthlessness that have been seen as key to business for too long will fade along with the 'old boys' club' behaviours. There have been notably good men who have been egalitarian and compassionate to all of their employees – for example, Mark Price, former managing director of Waitrose and deputy chairman of the John Lewis Partnership, and Tim Cook, CEO of Apple – but I think they have been the exceptions. Perhaps businesses would be more sustainable, and less vulnerable to lawsuits for discrimination and harassment, if there were more women in management and senior positions.

At the beginning of my career, I had a brush with sexual harassment. A famous British film director sat next to me at a polo match, started talking to me and seemed fascinated by my career. He said, 'I think we should meet to talk more about it.'

I felt flattered and optimistic that this connection could give me a boost somehow. But when I went back to the office and told colleagues what had happened, I got a weird feeling about it. Why would a sixty-year-old director be so interested in the career of a twenty-four-year-old junior publicist?

Before agreeing to meet him for lunch, I wrote him a letter (this was before email) that said, 'I'm so flattered by your invitation, but I just wanted to check that we'd be meeting for professional, not personal, reasons.'

His driver returned my letter with a red line through it, and a scribbled note from him: 'You shouldn't get married. Come with me instead.'

He was successful, older and confident in his power. I was just starting out, young, ambitious and recently engaged. If I hadn't listened to my inner voice and written the letter, I would have met him for lunch, wasted both of our time and possibly put myself in a compromising situation that might have had long-term emotional consequences.

Whenever there is an imbalance of power – across genders, orientations, ages and races – there is a potential for abuse. My approach to balance the scales back then was to write a polite note. It was surprisingly effective. I didn't get a career boost from this man (not that I would have anyway), but I felt very good about expressing my terms and standing by them.

If we've learned anything in the last couple of years about workplace abuses, it's that they can't always be stopped with a nice note. Women just want to do their job, and get paid (equally) for it, without having to deal with toxic swatting and commenting. It's really quite simple. And yet, we must still fight for this basic right not to be harassed. In November 2018, tens of thousands of Google employees of all genders walked off the job and protested about a number of anti-woman issues beyond just gender pay and promotion gaps, such as the company rewarding harassers with generous exit packages. Andy Rubin, the creator of Android, was accused of sexually assaulting a female employee. Google found the claim credible and gave him a $90 million severance package when he left. The protestors hoped to end Google's policy of requiring female accusers to file complaints privately to be arbitrated in-house and forcing them to waive their right to sue.

Although the protest was well reported and applauded in the tech world and mainstream media, it might not have done much to change the culture at the company. Two of the female protest organizers claimed that Google retaliated against them by demoting them and scrapping their projects.[8] They believe they've been punished for trying to effect change. The idea that anyone who tries to stand up for herself is then punished for it makes me incredibly sad. But I'm also hopeful that these stories are being told and the wrongdoers are being exposed.

The lessons of #MeToo have been very useful for both men and women in dealing with abuses of power in business. Awareness is the key. Men need to know what abuse looks like; women need to prick up their antennae for any hint of it. Instinctively, most of us know when things aren't quite right, don't we? If there is any question mark about a meeting or interaction, seek explicit, written clarification. Although it's not fair that women have to be vigilant, they should take care not to put themselves in any situation that has the faintest whiff of trouble. My style is to be non-confrontational but direct. For example, if a woman is at a bar or pub with colleagues, and a boss or person in power suggests going to his apartment or hotel room for further discussion, I'd recommend saying, 'That's not for me. It's inappropriate and I'd prefer to stay here.' These days, the word 'inappropriate' does a lot of work. It's code for 'potentially actionable'.

Pre-#MeToo, women weren't too keen to tell HR departments about the abuses they suffered and, if they did, they might have faced a backlash or been ignored. One month after Philip Green was exposed for his sexual (and racial) harassment, we learned that Ray Kelvin, the CEO of Ted Baker, the UK fashion chain with 544 outlets worldwide, had been forced to resign from the company he founded when 300 employees signed a petition accusing him of 'forced hugging', ear-kissing/massaging, neck-stroking, taking off his shirt and divulging details about his sex life, asking female staffers to sit on his knee, sexual innuendo and asking female employees for sex. [9,10] When employees complained to HR over many years, they were told to ignore Kelvin's behaviour, which was why they took it upon themselves to create a petition via the campaign website Organize to protest the culture of harassment at the retail chain.

If HR doesn't help, women know that they have options, like that petition. Or by taking to the Internet (like Susan Fowler, the woman who exposed Uber as a hostile work environment in a blog post), or by filing a lawsuit like TV host Gretchen Carlson at Fox News that ultimately lead to the downfall of CEO and chairman Roger Ailes. Technology has made it easier for women to collect evidence. I encourage any employee who is being abused in any way to keep electronic and hard copies of any offensive correspondence – texts, emails, voicemails. Document any conversation if you can genuinely anticipate a bad scene so you have a record of it. It's awful to have to be in a bad situation at all, but if you are, take precautions and get proof.

As the leader, I watch closely for any tiny abuses of power in the TCS universe, and if I do notice something, I seek to correct it immediately. For example, when a client was swearing and acting aggressively with some of our staffers, I rang him immediately and told him he could never speak to TCS staff that way again, or he could find another agency. He got the point and cleaned up his act.

Keep It Light

A boss is an authority figure, but that doesn't mean they're not human beings as well. Unless their natural personality is dry and humourless, a leader can and should make work-appropriate jokes at the office, especially if they're at their own expense. (FYI: The ability to laugh at oneself is a sign of higher intelligence, so use it to impress colleagues at will.)

I try to remind everyone in our office to keep it light and I do what I can to inject some humour into our days. A few Easters ago, I asked our head of creative to dress up in a Daddy Bunny suit, I dressed up in the Mummy Bunny suit, a senior leader was in the Teenage Bunny suit and our head of beauty's two gorgeous children, Violet and Ivy, aged seven and nine, were the Baby Bunnies. We hid in a room and then jumped out and ran all around the office distributing Easter eggs. When I took my bunny head off to show that it was me, people were doubled over laughing. It was just super *fun*. There is a video. It hasn't popped up on our Instagram. Every year now people take it upon themselves to put the suits on and hand out some chocolate.

A stodgy, too-formal office does nothing to inspire or excite anyone, so I like to try to breathe life and laughter into ours – and love, too, the unconditional kind. We British are obsessed with our pets, perhaps bordering on crazy. We have three poodles – two standards, named Lupa and Nana (think Peter Pan), and a miniature, Bertie – and I love them to bits. I often sit at my desk and imagine my husband at home with the dogs and I get back to centre, to my heart! I know our staff feels the same way, so pets are allowed to come to work. Having the animals around also reduces stress and fills the place with good vibes. One of our clients, Celia Forner, always brings her dog to meetings. He jumps on my lap while we're discussing strategy for her brand, ALLEVEN, and when he licks my face, I feel like it's his way of telling Celia that I'm okay.

Too often, people veer towards intensity at work. They care about the job, and that's good, but when someone ramps up the stakes too high, they need a leader who can change their perspective. My business partner Daniel Marks is my personal hero of inspiring calm in the office. There is a lot of hysteria and pressure in PR, as there is in every business. People can feel overwhelmed by a deadline and go a little crazy. Daniel has a way of quieting nerves and keeping things in perspective. As he tells our colleagues, 'You're in PR and communications with beautiful products, places and people. You're not a brain surgeon. No one is going to live or die over this pitch.' When someone at work needs a reality check about the stakes of what we do, they get it.

Be Grateful

In a memorable scene from *Mad Men*, a TV show that taught us so much about the traditional, 'masculine' way of doing business, the ad agency boss, Don Draper, and his young writer, Peggy Olson, were having a heated discussion about credit. She came up with the ad that won Draper an award, and he never publicly or privately acknowledged her contribution.

She said, 'You never say thank you.'

His reply? 'That's what the money is for!' Later, he said, 'You should be thanking *me* every morning when you wake up, along with Jesus, for giving you another day.'[11]

That would place Don Draper firmly in the BS category.

A secure leader recognizes the great work of their staff and doesn't think that expressing gratitude makes them any less of an authority figure or leader. I say 'thank you' and 'I appreciate you' a hundred times a day. It's not hard to do! I'd feel awful if we didn't let our staff know that we're grateful.

Employees work day after day at full throttle. How can a boss not be humbled with gratitude? At TCS, we go beyond words to show our appreciation with office perks (yoga classes, subsidised manicures, free smoothies and snacks), along with other benefits and remuneration. When one of our most trusted and senior leaders got married, we tried to do a little through our incredible client portfolio to make their honeymoon magical. The email I got from her husband afterwards was so kind and warm, it touched me beyond words. When another staffer was going through a devastating series of IVF treatments, we gave her paid leave. It was the least we could do for her family, considering her years of hard work for the company.

Every year, we have our annual Christmas party awards ceremony and give out a dozen or so honours, like Most Compassionate or Most Clever, to the staffers we want to give particular recognition to for their hard work all year. The winners get a bottle of champagne and an award. Daniel and I also love our holiday and summer parties for everyone, with good food and drink, little gifts and music. They're just another fun, heartfelt way to say thanks to all the staff.

Give People Their Space

Great leaders respect personal boundaries. You have to give people their space. If a boss crosses those lines by calling people constantly or demanding they stay at the office for unreasonable hours, they are not valuing care and kindness. A boss's 'be available at all times!' mandate actually decreases the quality of employees' work. A 2017 Gallup report found that overstressed, undervalued employees had 37 per cent higher absenteeism, 49 per cent more accidents, 60 per cent more errors and defects, 18 per cent lower productivity, 16 per cent lower profitability and 37 per cent lower job growth.[12]

There is no upside to burning people out. At BS offices, workaholic 'pacesetter' bosses demand that their staff not leave until they do and send urgent emails all night and over the weekend that must be replied to ASAP. Calling someone at home at midnight with an urgent 'do this or you're fired' message is an abuse of power. Now, if there is a really pressing deadline and all hands are required on deck, then yes, some personal hours and weekends will have to be sacrificed. I find it really hard to tolerate people letting work go unfinished on a Friday over and over again. But unless there is a very good reason to interfere with someone's life during off hours, we do not do it. Established ground rules must be observed. If I choose to work over the weekend, I very often use the 'send later' tab in Outlook. Tons of emails arrive at 9 a.m. on Monday, but not over the weekend unless really necessary.

Some companies, Google for example, have been accused of 24/7 food and nap pods to keep their employees working round the clock. For us, workplace sustainability means keeping a close eye on workflow and work stream. I don't want to see anyone working more than nine or ten hours a day. If we notice someone coming in at six in the morning and staying until midnight, we address it. I don't want them to work that hard and I will send tired people home. We all need our downtime and our rest!

Encourage Failure

A leader who fears innovation is doomed to fail. Sad to say, the 100-plus-year-old camera and film company Kodak filed for bankruptcy in 2012 after coming in too-little-too-late to the digital camera revolution. Ironically, a Kodak engineer was the first to design a digital camera back in 1975, but the company's leaders at the time decided not to sell it because they feared, rightly, that a digital camera would decimate its film business. By the time they realized digital was going to replace film, they'd already missed their chance. Japanese companies Canon and Fuji got there first and dominated the market.[13] A similar fumble happened at Xerox when they developed the first personal computer and the CEO shelved the idea, believing the future of the company was in photocopiers. The former CEO of Blockbuster Video, John Antioco, turned down a deal to partner with Netflix in 2000, calling the DVD-by-mail company a 'niche business'. If Blockbuster had agreed to Netflix CEO Reed Hastings' offer, it might still be operating in some capacity today.

A leader has to be brave enough to take risks and to encourage their staff to try new ideas and approaches. Any leader that plays it safe by saying, 'This is how things are always done' or 'We're doing just fine the way we are' won't be so safe or fine for long. When James Quincey took over as CEO of Coca-Cola in 2017, he was walking into a company in decline, one that had been burned by a bad mistake with the disastrous product launch of New Coke. He told his team, 'If we're not making mistakes, we're not trying hard enough.'[14] It remains to be seen if his mistake-making policy will increase sales, but I like his attitude.

Simon Sinek, author of *Leaders Eat Last* and a TED Talk genius (his lecture 'How great leaders inspire action' has been viewed nearly 44 million times), once said to me something like, 'It's crazy isn't it, when a leader fires someone for making one mistake. If your kid does something wrong at home, you don't immediately put them up for adoption, do you? You wrack your brain as to why they might have made a bad decision and then you do all you can to discipline them, show them the right path, help them make better decisions.' Many BS bosses clearly take a different tack and haven't yet gone to the school of Simon Sinek.

Society's entire concept of success has to be revised. Perfection is an unobtainable goal that cannot and should not be aspired to. At school, no one scores a perfect 100 per cent on every test (and if you did, you really need to get out more). People mess up now and again. It's part of being human. We fail so we can learn, and yet, some bosses punish staff for failing. In a BS toxic environment, employees will most likely develop an 'omission bias', leaning towards not bringing new, innovative ideas to the boss for fear of failure hurting their reputation or leading to some kind of punishment.

It seems unethical for a leader to fire or demote staffers for failure and/or foist blame and shame on them for making human errors. Office politics in general (and finger-pointing in particular) will not inspire greatness. It only inspires fear. Blaming is a conditioned response; if covering one's tracks is standard BS protocol, people will do it in order to survive. Improvement and growth are beside the point. A fearful staff will adapt to avoid any action that might bring down the boss's wrath.

Not only do ethical leaders avoid an accusatory tone, they keep an ear open for any hint of it from others. If I ever hear someone in a more senior position blaming a junior person, big alarm bells ring instantly. 'Your juniors are managed by you, nurtured by you, guided by you, so what would the reason be for you to throw them under the bus?' I ask. 'What can we do together to teach people, and learn from what happened?' And then I ask them to collaborate on an innovative solution to the problem. And when they do, I thank them for the effort and it normally has a positive outcome.

Be Open to Criticism

At TCS we believe in a 360-degree perspective on ourselves. Every year, we ask the staff to fill out anonymous surveys through *The Sunday Times* Best Small 100 Companies awards. These awards are incredible to win, but actually serve us even better by telling us honestly how staffers feel about the office culture and all aspects of their jobs. One question on the survey is: 'In terms of management style and leadership, what could the CEO do better?' Since I take care to be authentic and honest, speak deliberately, give clear direction and mind my language, I hoped that my staff wouldn't have much to say about my communications style. I thought they understood me completely. And I was wrong.

According to the survey results, some staffers said they would like me to be 'easier to read and less intimidating'. I thought I was communicating clarity and approachability all along! One person mentioned my inscrutable, and therefore intimidating, 'thinking face'. I thought I was being gentle by keeping my expression calm at all times. Some said I was *too* generous in my praise and not angry when I should have been, that I did not actually express my dissatisfaction openly enough. They wanted me to be a bit more brutal, honest. Well, I had set out to be the opposite of the abusive bosses I'd worked for in the past, so, to a degree... mission accomplished! Daniel jokes with our team about the colour of the frames of my almost infamous glasses. My reading glasses come in a variety of colours. He says they are quite symbolic and wonders if I choose my white-rimmed fierce glasses for the tougher days!

I'll be honest – some of the feedback from staff really hurts and can be brutal. But however much it hurts, it is often right. I know that from the toughest moments in my career, I've learned the most. Challenge and difficulty are good for us. They make us better at what we do and who we are. If only every company, boss and co-worker received some kind of insightful, valuable feedback about how they come off to their colleagues, via surveys, online forums or even a suggestion box. I welcome anonymous feedback because it's *honest*, but I also like open discussion in any form or forum. Recently, two of our staff members started a forum in the office called 'TCS Voice'. It's literally that – a place for staff to come together, discuss things, make changes and vent.

Leaders would be more mindful about the intricacies of interpersonal communications if they knew how they affected people. But, sadly, many companies and leaders don't prioritize or invest in insight. They just plod along and try to ignore the reality of work – that how people interact with each other, and how they communicate their thoughts and feelings, really does matter.

If leaders are unaware of or uncaring about their employee feedback, they're missing the opportunity to improve. It's not possible to bury one's head in the sand and hope that criticism just disappears. In the age of accountability that we have thankfully entered, no one should be able to get away with treating people badly. BS behaviour will be exposed, and leaders will have to explain themselves and make necessary changes.

JUST DO YOUR BEST

You can't control how people react to you. Assumptions will be made. Blanks will be filled in. Even if you, as a boss, supervisor or junior person, are following all the no-BS principles I've mentioned, it is entirely possible you will be misunderstood. People prove themselves over time and through shared experience. If you are consistently compassionate and ethical, people will come to see you as trustworthy and kind. Just keep doing your best, and hoping for the best.

Reward Talent and Accomplishment

In 2016, the American pizza franchise Papa John's was a market leader with 5000 stores and $1.7 billion in revenue. Then an in-depth investigation of the company alleged that former CEO John Schnatter encouraged employees to spy on one another and report back to him, and that he was secretly reading staffers' emails.[15] Schnatter made at least two confidential settlements with female employees over his alleged inappropriate conduct. Many former and current Papa John's employees have accused him of commenting on women's bodies and appearances, and asking about their sexual histories, availability and preferences. When he made public derogatory comments about black Americans, including use of the 'N-word' on a conference call, the stock price promptly plummeted and Schnatter was forced to resign as chairman.

In a PR nightmare like this, the smart move would have been to appoint a new CEO who would represent a change in the company culture away from insensitivity and harassment, towards respect and inclusiveness. Papa John's went another way. Top posts had long been filled with Schnatter's personal friends and loyalists over more qualified, talented people. His successor as CEO, a man named Steve Ritchie, was one of Schnatter's old friends and has been accused of incompetence and sexual misconduct himself, although he denied all the allegations after they were published in *Forbes*. He has not led the struggling company to recovery. At the time of writing, profits are down 40 per cent, with no bottom in sight.

I've noticed the unfortunate practice of leaders promot-ing and hiring people because of a personal friendship or a sense of loyalty. The most egregious example of this BS boss style is President Donald Trump, who hires family members and friends, and fires anyone he perceives as disloyal to him *personally*. Nepotism and cronyism might give an insecure boss a sense of security, that they are surrounded by people who will protect them, but hiring and promoting less qualified friends over talented people hurts the company at large. A wise leader has to think about the bigger picture, not just their own comfort.

A magazine editor friend told me this story about one of her favourite bosses:

I'd been working at the magazine for seven years and had risen to be the head of my department. A manager job came up and I just assumed, given my seniority and the close friendship I'd developed with my boss, that I'd get it. My boss called me into her office and calmly informed me that the job had gone to one of my colleagues instead. I sat there stunned. She explained, 'You are a great writer and editor. That's what you do best. You're not a natural manager of people but your colleague is. I'm sorry if you're disappointed, but you are better where you are.'

I sulked for three days. And then I realized she was right. I didn't want to manage people, and tell them what to do, be responsible for them, nurture and guide them, nag them about deadlines and give them annual reviews. I was happy in my role. I respected my boss even more for doing the right thing for the magazine, and for telling me first, which couldn't have been easy for her. Once I saw the wisdom of her decision, I was able to celebrate my colleague's promotion and embrace my own role wholeheartedly.

A no-BS boss values each employee for what they have to offer. They can recognize unique talents while ignoring personal connections and favouritism, and do what's best for the company at large. Promotions should go to the most deserving. Full stop.

Empower Women

In our early days, Tom and I used to go to client meetings together. Too often, the (usually male) client would speak only to him. I never felt the need to say, 'Excuse me. I'm Julietta Dexter, the CEO and founder of the company.' We wanted their business and I didn't think putting myself forward would help. One client ignored me for the length of our meeting and, at its conclusion, said, 'Nice to meet you Tom. But, tell me, why did you bring your assistant?' In his mind, any woman in a meeting had only one purpose: to support the men. In all fairness, back in the mid-1990s, he might never have met a female businesswoman before.

In leadership roles, women are still a rare breed. According to 2018 stats from *Fortune* magazine's annual list of the top 500 US companies, only twenty-four of them are helmed by a woman, a hair less than 5 per cent overall.[16] According to a report by the Lean In organization and McKinsey & Company, since 2015, the first year of this study, 'The proportion of women at every level in corporate America has hardly changed. Progress isn't just slow. It's stalled.'[17] For every 100 men promoted to a manager position, only seventy-nine women are. Only 23 per cent of senior VPs in Fortune 500 companies are women. What's more, 55 per cent of women who have had the fortitude to reach the top claim to have been sexually harassed on their way up. Often, these strong women feel ganged up on as the only woman in the room.

In the UK, the female leadership picture is only slightly better. According to one report, as of 2018, in the FTSE 100 there are just six female CEOs, or 6 per cent.[18] The Chartered Institute of Personnel and Development and the High Pay Centre put out an amusing finding, that there were more CEOs in the FTSE 100 named David or Steve (eight of each) than there were women in that position.[19]

There is one very fast way to change the dismal percentages of women in leadership and management dramatically: any male executive who has discriminated against, harassed or assaulted a female staffer should be fired and replaced by a woman. As someone who has made it one of her missions to empower and promote women in the workplace, I am doing what I can to fill the pipeline with talent. Perhaps if every woman in management and leadership does the same, we will make progress. Given the past hundreds of years of history, we can't expect men to help us too much.

When I read articles about the imbalance of women in leadership, I admit that I get a little angry, which is not an emotion I'm completely comfortable with. I'd rather not have to get mad, ever, but when I look at the challenges of being a boss and woman/mother/wife, it's inevitable. Being a woman, having kids and being a good mum is hard alongside having a massive career. It is not for everyone. And no woman should be judged for realizing that and having a professional life that suits her. Many women do not want to be the CEO and they should not, and to that end we should not pretend that women and men are the same. Controversial, but true.

One finding in the Lean In/McKinsey study that I found fascinating in this light was that the reason so few women are in leadership roles is not necessarily because they quit to have children or work fewer hours because of family responsibilities. It's due to an unconscious bias against them. Sheryl Sandberg, COO of Facebook, author of *Lean In* and founder of the eponymous organization, wrote in *The Wall Street Journal* recently, 'We expect men to be assertive, look out for themselves, and lobby for more, so there's little downside when they do it. But women must be communal and collaborative, nurturing and giving, focused on the team and not themselves, lest they be viewed as self-absorbed. So when a woman advocates for herself, people often see her unfavourably.'[20]

To Sandberg, perhaps the solution to the bias against empowered women is to be less kind and caring. I can't see that as a solution. But we do need to point out casual acts of sexism when we see them, even if it does come off as brash. At a business dinner, I was seated next to the CEO of a large apparel company, and he talked at me for an hour and a half. I asked him twenty-nine questions about politics, his business, his family. He didn't ask me one single question, despite the fact that I've run my own successful business for a quarter of a century, and that I also had opinions about Brexit and the future of retail. At the end of the meal, I asked him one more question: 'We have been talking for quite some time and you haven't asked for my opinion about anything we've discussed. Is it because you think you have more to contribute and more wisdom to offer than I do?' His face paled slightly, and then he got up and walked away.

I don't think I got through to him... but I am committed to my subtle war against 'mansplaining' whenever I come into contact with it.

The values of giving and collaboration are exactly what we cherish – and promote – at TCS as our greatest strength. That said, I do feel torn about how women can perhaps take one or two stereotypically 'male' qualities and speak up for themselves a bit more forcefully. I feel strongly that business people should be *more* caring and cooperative, and yet, these same qualities might hold back women in a traditional male-oriented corporate culture.

The answer to this quandary is certainly not to be *less* kind and collaborative! However, women can and should advocate passionately for themselves and for other women. We should be seen and heard, in greater numbers, at every level, at every age. And get tougher.

At the Founders Forum conference one year, I heard the brilliant Dame Carolyn McCall give a speech about her experiences as a CEO. McCall has had some very impressive jobs in her past, as a director at Burberry, the chief executive at the *Guardian* and the CEO of easyJet, and was named in 2017 as the CEO of ITV. I'd met her previously and felt like we had a similar outlook on leadership. Some of her advice to up-and-comers matches my own: get to know your colleagues, customers and clients to better understand their needs and desires, love what you do which makes you more enjoyable to work with and play to your strengths while filling in the gaps of your weaknesses as best you can.

While listening to her speak at that panel, I was struck by her overall demeanour and tone of quiet confidence. She's just a damn fine business person. I know from personal experience that whenever a female CEO sits in front of a room for a Q&A, someone in the audience will ask how she manages to 'have it all'. McCall just did not go there. She talked about her career and how she built a budget airline, as well as the future of TV in the UK. Never once did she mention the challenges of being a boss and a mum, or how her femaleness might've hindered her rise. She skirted (as it were) the entire issue of gender and just spoke about how she got where she is.

What I hope and pray for is a future where people of every race, sexuality and gender come to the workplace to be creative and rigorous, where people with the best skills are doing the right jobs. I'm hugely optimistic for this vision. If I asked my daughter, 'Does your friend John have more of a chance of being a CEO than you do?' I'm sure she'd reply, 'That's ridiculous' or, better, in my younger daughter Darcy's language, 'Oh, grow up.' I was raised in a traditional home where my father was the boss. My daughters have been raised in a home where their mother in some ways was perceived as taking on the 'father' role. As far as they know, it's only natural for women to lead.

I've taken a cue from Carolyn and decided that I'm done talking about the challenges of being a mother or a woman and a CEO. My being female is beside the point. I have made choices as a business person, a mother, a wife, that work for me. If I inspire anyone at all, it'll be because of how I operate, what I do and what I believe in. I run our business partially with my feminine skills – intuition, compassion, empathy – but that is just being true to my personal style and how I serve best. Kindness and collaboration are what I used to bake our company from scratch, and I'm proud of how well it's risen.

Don't Be Afraid to Make Tough Decisions

To plan for the long-term health and viability of our company as a whole, we have had to cut our losses on occasion. Letting people go is always difficult, even when it's completely justified.

Our employment policy follows the market standard for a company of our size, as the law mandates. Step one is to give a verbal warning, which I often issue myself. If someone is doing something that takes advantage of or is in direct conflict with our staff policies, they will be put on notice. Should there be more offences, the next step would be to issue the person with a written warning, followed by a final written warning and then a dismissal.

After the first written warning, we do offer to set up a performance improvement plan for those who just need closer supervision and support. But in most cases we have already made the job requirements and objectives quite clear, and going over them ad nauseam isn't going to make much difference if someone is a bad fit, just isn't up to the demands of the job or has been grossly negligent. Whatever the circumstances, people are let go with respect and care. Even when I might have reason to be annoyed with someone we've had to dismiss, I still treat them fairly and hope they will go on to shine brightly somewhere else. In the process, I think about how I would want to be spoken to if I was in the other person's shoes.

Once in a half-decade, we have an unredeemable personality problem, and those are the redundancies that rob me of my sleep. When you fire a person who has the skills but not the temperament for your company culture, it could be a bumpy exit. They might take to social media and their networks to trash us. Anyone who would do that to us isn't a good fit for our culture anyway, and the departure, however difficult, was the right call for them, and for us.

As tough as those conversations are for me, it's not about me. I'm ever mindful that the person across from me is losing their job, taking a massive blow to their ego, facing uncertainty, worrying about what to say about it at home, stressing about the next mortgage payment, and so on. Our HR director is usually sitting in the room as well, and she's taught me a lot about how to demonstrate compassion but not regret in this delicate situation.

I don't BS around the issue or soften the blow by telling someone how wonderful they are and how sorry I am. Research shows that people do not like humming and hawing. In a 2017 study, a linguistics professor from Brigham Young University recruited 145 participants and asked them to choose between two approaches – a slow wind-up or a bombshell drop – to receiving bad news in a handful of scenarios, such as getting fired, being dumped, finding out you have a serious illness, etc.[21] Overwhelmingly, the subjects preferred the direct approach, describing it as clear, considerate and honest, many of the words that define a no-BS leadership style.

Whenever a senior person leaves the company, considering our position in some very glamorous industries, tongues wag. Customarily, BS companies issue a fake-sounding press release that says so-and-so has decided to leave the company to 'spend more time with their family', or something similarly unbelievable. While I understand the merits of compromised agreements, I think everybody can see right through the code. So why bother pushing the 'company line' if no one believes it?

One time, I had to make a very difficult decision about the future of our business. A very senior leader had been a loyal friend, confidante and mentor for eleven years, but the company was growing and evolving with new technology and into new areas. I felt, rightly or wrongly, that we needed someone with international experience and who had worked in businesses bigger than ours. At times, I suggested moving the company on and doing things differently, but she bristled against making any changes. I realized that I was asking somebody to go beyond what she believed in and where she felt comfortable. I made the hideous decision to make her role redundant and put this wonderful person with kids out of a job after more than a decade of love and loyalty. But I knew that the company had to change, evolve and transform, and she didn't.

As a leader, you sometimes have to make hard decisions that affect people's lives. I had her life to consider, but also the lives of the 200 other people on the payroll, as well as being mindful of the strategic vision of the company.

I did all we could to pay her fairly and honour her for her length of service and loyalty. After we discussed how she wanted me to explain the situation to the rest of the staff, the two of us stood up in front of the whole company side by side. She and I both wanted to be honest, and avoid the 'more time with family' line. I said, 'I have made this decision. This is my responsibility. I believe that, for the future of our company and our community, this good person is no longer the right person to hold this role. We've come to a financial settlement with her to look after her and her family. Will you join me in wishing her good luck, and to thank her for everything that she's done to take our company to where it is today?' It was an excruciating day for all of us. But it was the truth. We keep in touch regularly. The only way to do unpleasant jobs is to walk the walk, take full responsibility and handle the situation with empathy, honesty and kindness, as best I can. And then I go in my office, close the door and let my emotion out, in private.

Being a no-BS leader really comes down to one overriding principle: bring out the best in people by being a good example of ethical, compassionate values, even while doing the dirty work. In any decision or plan of action, a fearless leader does what is best for everyone besides themselves, because in the end, having a happy and engaged workforce is all the proof they need that they're doing the job to the best of their abilities.

LEADERSHIP

To paraphrase President John F. Kennedy, a good leader doesn't ask what you can do for the company, but what the company can do for you. In a no-BS office, the answers are the same.

- Find and appreciate the value and talent in every employee, whether they're young, old, male, female, or other.
- Promote talented hard workers.
- Prevent abuses of power with awareness. Supervisors need to know what behaviours are offensive and actionable, and they must be held accountable; workers need to report incidents and gather proof when possible.
- A boss should be a source of calm and give people a necessary dose of perspective when things get tense.
- Inject humour into the work day... just because. The load is lighter when you're laughing.
- You can't say 'thank you' enough!
- Respect people's boundaries, and don't call or email over the weekend or late at night. Everyone, including the boss, needs downtime.
- As a leader, if you do your best, you'll inspire others to do theirs.
- Leadership is a privilege. Never take it for granted. Be humble, always.

2 Culture

Nearly every company and organization spells out its mission on its website. For example:

> The American Heart Association defines their culture with the keywords 'integrity, excellence, vision, dedication, inclusiveness, sensitivity'.[1]
>
> The World Wildlife Fund: 'results, integrity and respect'.[2]
>
> Coca-Cola: 'leadership, collaboration, integrity, accountability, passion, diversity, quality'.[3]
>
> Marriott's official mission statement says they put people first and embrace change, along with 'excellence, integrity and service'.[4]

From such diverse companies, you can see the recurring themes. What company, large or small, for-profit or charitable, *wouldn't* uphold the values of quality, excellence, integrity and respect? You are unlikely to read a corporate mission statement that boasts about the company's commitment to mediocrity, ordinariness, corruption and antipathy. The mission statements of the new generation of tech and more holistic companies are specific and detailed about what they actually do and are therefore more relevant and (perhaps) believable. For example:

> Google's famous 'ten things we know to be true' list includes: 'Focus on the user; it's better to do one thing really, really well; fast is better than slow; you can make money without doing evil; you can be serious without a suit; great just isn't good enough.'[5]
>
> Whole Foods is committed to providing quality natural and organic products, customer satisfaction and delight, team member happiness and growth, profit and prosperity, environment stewardship and to serve and support the local community.[6]

When I read a company's list of core values, I take them with a pinch of salt. To a large extent, these statements are akin to press releases only intended to promote the company rather than a product. The key words are so predictable that they're essentially empty. That's why the foundation of PR is really interesting to me. You can say what you like about yourself (which is what advertising does), but the proof is in what people say back about you.

Therefore, a core values statement is only as good as a company's willingness to live up to it. Facebook's stated core values are 'be bold and open, focus on impact, build social value' and its famous internal motto was 'move fast and break things'.[7] Perhaps Facebook has been too fast and loose with exploiting users' data and broken public confidence in the company.

Although some hot air might be whistling through corporate core values statements, the passion behind them rings more strongly. If I were just starting out in my career or looking for my next mid- to high-level job, I would gravitate towards a company with a compassionate culture that serves the community and protects the environment. To paraphrase Google's 'great isn't good enough', 'excellence' and 'integrity' aren't good enough either. A company's values might be innovative, specific and inspiring, but it's all about how it lives up to them. When you hear employees saying that such-and-such a company is a great place to work, that really impresses me.

Create Core Values

At TCS many years ago, I chose four core values I was confident I could really try to live up to and wanted to dedicate myself to. These were the 'C's of The Communications Store: we should try to be clever, considered, considerate and maybe even a little counter-cultural in all that we did and said. I like these words and use them a lot. A few years ago, we worked with an external consultant to check that these words were still truly relevant to the evolving business. The leadership team came up with words that, in my mind, are different but essentially the same: strength, wisdom, passion and care. We've made these the main job requirement of our staff and the secret to our success.

Strength

We always rely on what we're good at. It's valuable for an individual to know what they're uniquely good at so they can work with confidence, do wonders and feel excited about their contributions. For example, one of the many strengths of my former business partner, Tom, is his extraordinary personal charm. He is magnetic and has a way of making everyone his immediate life-long friend. You meet Tom, and you've met an out-of-the-ordinary human being and your life is enhanced. My strength is more on the analytical, strategic side of things, to puzzle through problems. Tom and I worked together to our strengths and developed new ones by learning from each other. Strength also means having the fortitude to play the long game and gain, not taking the easy route, not compromising your values for the sake of another bit of revenue. Finally, it's about standing strong, not being pushed around and staying true to yourself.

Wisdom

... or good judgement wrought from intelligence and experience. To inhabit this value, one must be as informed and inventive as possible, and always keep an open mind. We live in suggestible times, where if one person says something, others tend to just parrot it back without scrutinizing it. The world has enough followers. If people use their brains and question the current zeitgeist, they will come up with unconventional ideas that are the lifeblood of any creative and sustainable business. At TCS, we're always striving to have the data and the insight to understand what's relevant and important, to tune out noise and to know what will make a difference and will move the needle for us, our clients and our larger agenda. Our real purpose is to make positive change.

Passion

We expect our people to really love the products we promote, the industry we're in and their particular role within the company. If someone is only lukewarm about what they're doing, then we discuss it and move them to another position that they can get excited about. If we don't feel passion about some aspect of the work, we share our misgivings and reservations with the client (resulting in some very awkward but necessary conversations) and collaborate with them to fix it or go our separate ways. It's hard for anyone to be authentic without passion. One of the greatest professional blessings is to have the luck or the judgement to find a job that inspires fire in the belly.

Care

Care is two-fold. It means doing a job with attention to detail and consideration. By taking care, people are more emotionally invested in their work. The second part of 'care' is kindness and empathy, caring about how people feel. I care deeply about every aspect of the business, on a personal and professional level. If I didn't, I wouldn't hold our clients to a higher standard than average and raise tough questions, like, 'Does the world really need another night cream?' To care means *not* spinning a story but speaking truth. Caring is living by one's values rather than being controlled only by profit. When I talk about how much I care about the staff at TCS, I actually feel a lump in my throat. Everything is vastly more meaningful with emotional connection.

Strength, wisdom, passion and care are the threads that run through everything we do at TCS. Having a unified philosophy makes everything easier. I agree with Tony Hsieh, CEO of online retail shoe store Zappos, who told the *New York Times* in 2010, 'We really view culture as our No. 1 priority. We decided that if we get the culture right, most of the stuff, like building a brand around delivering the very best customer service, will just take care of itself.'[8]

When choosing where to work or when creating a company of your own, the first order of business is to figure out the philosophy. What do you believe in? What do you stand for? How do you want to manifest those values at work? Composing a corporate culture wish list doesn't have to be a long-winded essay; just a few key words are enough to guide a jobseeker or aspiring CEO towards like-minded people and businesses. I respect and admire job applicants when they steer the interview towards our culture. If they've done their homework – as all wise candidates should have – they already know our values. By showing that they share them, we can move forward in our discussion with simpatico.

When we set out to define TCS's values, we chose words that resonated powerfully within me and my partners and would appeal to the kind of people we hoped to bring in. Over the last few decades, we've refined our corporate culture and have added more words to the list: humility, collaboration, inclusion and relationships. Values grow and evolve; each person's list of key words is not set in stone.

Each of our values is distinct as we interpret and manifest them, but they are pieces of the same compassionate pie.

We work together, listen to each other, trust and take care to strengthen our bonds. Compassion is the glue that holds us together.

According to a study by researchers at the Wharton School of Business at the University of Pennsylvania of over 3200 workers in seven different professional fields, those in offices with a 'culture of compassionate love' – where people can express their feelings, be appropriately affectionate and caring with colleagues – were happier, more committed and accountable for their performance compared to those who worked in emotionally buttoned-up (BS) professional environments.[9]

That's not to say that the values of a 'cognitive culture' and a compassionate culture are mutually exclusive. You certainly couldn't stay in business for long without intellect, innovation and hard work. But in an empathetic office, people take special care to tend to feelings, too.

Years ago, I outlined our emotional culture in a PowerPoint presentation entitled 'How we feel it' and have since shown it to all new staffers as part of their orientation process. Slides include items such as, really listen; don't accept bullying, ever; acknowledge and accept; kindness; smile; don't judge; accountability; and honesty. Of course, you can't mandate how someone feels, but I do expect employees to conduct their interactions with these empathetic guidelines in mind. It all goes towards ensuring that people feel heard, safe and supported. In general, how we treat each other as human beings is critical to our culture and our success. The traditional separation of the personal and professional – manifested in colleagues keeping each other at an emotional distance – seems heartless and unrealistic to me. Trying to remove humanity from business is what causes unethical BS behaviour in the first place. The world needs to move to a different, more empathetic place.

Many Minds Are Better Than One

A BS culture basic tenet is to create a sense of competition among colleagues. The idea being, if people are striving to beat each other, they will all do their best work. Not true, according to a fascinating study by Harvard Business School, Northeastern University and Boston University.[10] Study subjects were divided into three groups of three. Group A members worked independently and produced a high quantity of solutions to a problem, with a notable low quality (with a few exceptions). Group B members worked together constantly and came up with an average quantity of solutions of average quality as well. Consistently, the only-collaborative group failed to come up with the best solutions. Group C worked independently for a period of time followed by a period of collaboration and came up with an average quantity of solutions of consistently higher quality. Researchers concluded that 'intermittent collaboration', the pattern of working alone, then together, and so on, was the most productive.

Granted, some individuals work best alone and feel uncomfortable in a group setting. They need isolation to think. I have found that, in the context of our culture, we are most successful collaborating nearly all the time. Collaboration is in the DNA of our company. As soon as someone arrives, they are assigned to a team. The team can be any size. Each team might handle a specific account or aspect of a particular arm of the business, like beauty, lifestyle, finance or HR. Within each team, there are smaller partnerships of two or three, so no one person is alone on any task. Teams meet to brainstorm and troubleshoot. Team leaders attend weekly 'Working Together' sessions to discuss any number of issues, including personal beefs within or between teams. If there is an issue, we don't point fingers at one person and read them the riot act about how they have to change and improve. The question that goes around the table is and always should be, 'How are we going to solve this together? How can we help?'

REACH OUT

You might have grown up believing that asking for help is a sign of weakness. But being able to work collaboratively is only a strength. When you put aside ego and reach out to a colleague to tackle a problem together, you're more likely to fix it. Each person brings a fresh perspective and set of ideas. Too many times to count, I've been in meetings with clients, and one person on the team made a suggestion that someone else picked up and ran with. Whose contribution is greater: the one who set off the spark or the one who fanned it into a fire? In my mind, they are equally vital, and a must. In fact, in our biannual employee reviews, we evaluate people on their individual strength and also *as a team member*.

I understand that Google has invested millions analyzing group dynamics and what combinations of factors lead to the most effective teams. During a two-year study called Project Aristotle, researchers there discovered that the decisive factors weren't shared personality traits, IQ, experience or whether the team members were friends outside of work.[11] The best teams – the fastest innovators and problem-solvers – shared an understanding and respect for a 'group norm', aka its culture. What's more, the most successful norms were having clear goals, dependability and 'psychological safety', meaning that everyone in the group felt enthusiastic, free to contribute, relaxed and valued. Each team member was integral to the team effort, and comfortable about the process.

A friend who worked at a large ad agency in New York described pitching meetings as 'ritual execution'. She said:

People were required to present three ideas, but it was not an opportunity to shine. It felt like a competition for who could be the most wittily savage in destroying each other's ideas. The boss encouraged it because he felt that if an idea was still viable after a dozen smart people tried to dismantle it, then it was good. If thirty-six ideas were put forward, maybe three or four would get through the process. I remember walking out of those meeting needing a shower. I felt awful about being so mean, but if you didn't criticize an idea, the boss thought you were going soft or not smart enough to see its flaws. In hindsight, I know that if we'd worked towards building ideas instead of tearing them apart, we would have had a lot more options, and friendships, among us.

In a no-BS culture, any idea is a good idea. A toxic culture that fosters fear about making a contribution is counterproductive. As author Liz Wiseman wrote in her bestseller *Multipliers: How the Best Leaders Make Everyone Smarter*, when you encourage people to express themselves, their productivity and creativity multiplies, but when people feel ignored, intimidated or insulted, their output diminishes.[12]

However, even in a culture of psychological safety, there are pitfalls. According to an article in the *Harvard Business Review*, people who contribute the most resources to a group tend to do significantly more than their less-collaborative colleagues.[13] Nearly a third of 'value-added collaborations' are generated by only 3–5 per cent of employees, who tend to be women. In effect, those high-value women were carrying the load for the other 97–95 per cent of men and women. Why weren't the low-value people contributing their share? A whole host of reasons: they felt unappreciated; they were talked over or discounted (as per Wiseman's lexicon, 'diminished'); or they just had less to offer and figured, since the 'top collaborators' brought so much, they didn't have to show up at all.

For collaboration to work well, it must be evenly distributed. At TCS, we have managers to guide and steer a team, but each member is treated with the same compassion and respect, regardless of seniority. Unless junior people are encouraged to speak up and participate in the group effort, they won't feel ownership of it. Leaders make a point of asking their juniors what they think, and everyone gets a turn to talk.

If I sense that juniors are intimidated into silence by more experienced colleagues, I have a private word with them and say, 'We're just people with personalities, weaknesses, strengths, feelings. Even if a senior vice president is dressed head-to-toe in whatever designer, there's no need to be scared of her. She sits on the loo, just like you.'

I've been told that when I'm in the room, newer members of staff are less likely to be outspoken. I hate that. I sometimes walk into the room full of ideas about a project and ask the group to go out of their way to challenge me, build on my ideas and show me how their changes will make them better. Just because someone is young doesn't mean they have nothing to offer. They might have a perspective that we really need at that moment. Particularly in this digital age, younger people often know more about some things than those with age and experience. No matter how old, everyone's opinion has value. Which brings me to my next point about compassionate office culture...

Play on a Level Field, Not a Ladder

Our style of an egalitarian meritocracy would be frowned upon at many traditional companies. I remember writing a speech about benevolent leadership to present at the Paris headquarters of a famous jewellery brand at their annual marketing and sales meeting. In the speech, I suggested that by doing really simple things like making a receptionist or an entry-level person a coffee, or offering to do something for them, showed good leadership skills. The young woman who I was working with was amazed that a CEO would make coffee for an assistant, and I suggested that small gestures like this inspired loyalty among staff and earned a reputation as a compassionate boss.

The president of the jewellery brand reviewed my speech the day before the event and, to my surprise, he asked me to cut out the CEO-makes-coffee anecdote.

'Why don't you like that one?' I asked him.

'No senior person at my company is going to make a junior person coffee,' he said.

'That's not how we do things, and it never will be.'

He thought my talking about it would embarrass the senior people in the room because they treated the junior people so badly, a classic BS cultural 'pay your dues' hierarchy. I got the feeling that advocating common courtesy would cause a mutiny among the ranks. I can't imagine that anyone on the bottom rungs of that company feels tenderly towards management.

Some senior people are invested in the BS concept of seniority, the idea that anyone below them on the totem pole in the office is there to do their bidding, if they're worth acknowledging at all. Think of the kind of managers who refer to more junior members of staff as 'minions'.

I remember being in the kitchen at TCS's London office with some junior account execs, flipping through the newspapers. I wanted to share my insight from a PR perspective about certain articles, how to read a newspaper, what to look for, how to understand a journalist's particular point of interest and how to pitch a story to that journalist. One of the junior execs started laughing and said, 'At my last company, the CEO never knew I existed, and here you are, chatting about the news and teaching me how to do my job.'

What is the point of being a leader if you can't teach and serve those who are coming up around you? There is only one difference between you and them: you have just been in the workplace for a longer time. Being a leader is a privilege, not a divine right. It's up to those 'at the top' to inspire and bring out the leadership qualities in others, make sure they feel seen, heard and really appreciated. That is one of the purposes I serve. Hopefully, they, in turn, will pass along the validation to better serve each other and our clients.

CHALLENGE THE 'WAY THINGS ARE' WITH KINDNESS

Even if you work at a company with an established hierarchy, you can always demonstrate kindness and offer to help those closest to you. You might just inspire more of the same among your colleagues. What would happen if you did make coffee for your assistant, or partnered up with a colleague to brainstorm ideas, even if your company culture values go-it-alone individualism? You might upset and confound the powers that be. More likely, you'll win a new friend and, together, come up with a better strategy that your boss can only applaud.

Be Inclusive

I was reading an article in *The Economist* about the trend of women going on gender-exclusive Finnish island retreats for yoga, detox and networking or all-female social/professional clubs like The Allbright in London and The Wing in New York. I am a strong proponent of female empowerment and women helping women. I have lived by those principles every day of my career. But when I think about going to work at a place like The Wing, with its pink walls and scented bathrooms, I long for what's missing: men.

I completely understand the reasoning for creating female-friendly workspaces and networks where women won't feel over-powered or patronized by men. But my core belief is that we need to get to that idyllic safe, powerful, productive place by understanding each other's skills and capabilities by working together, irrespective of gender. Surely our objective should be to evolve past sexual problems in the workplace, towards gender equality. As a human being, I don't feel completely comfortable in exclusive environments because they don't aspire to that objective. Separate is not equal, either way. It's not sustainable.

This take is controversial, I know. And please don't think this means anyone should stop inviting me to female power summits, which I enjoy attending. But when the subject turns to man-bashing, I tune out. My two business partners, Tom and Daniel, have been incredible, inspiring men; between us, we have created a unique, powerful, creative dynamic in our office. It would also be wrong not to mention Mungo, my beloved husband. As a doting, caring, constant, unerring step-dad to Darcy and Valentina, this man has loved me, supported me, encouraged me, believed in me and listened to me, selflessly. Our chairman, John Hoffman, is also a great guide and leveller to me.

I love working with women. I love working with men. When we are all putting our minds and perspectives into the pot together, we come up with a strange, potent brew. I feel like the absence of men in the workplace and in leadership would be just as toxic as the lack of women has been historically.

What I don't want to see is any person underrepresented and underpaid because of the pronoun they use. And I'd love to see wise, wonderful women of all ages in equal number to their male counterparts throughout the business world. At TCS, we discuss representation and equality for people of *all* genders. The solution to such problems as abuses of power, sexual harassment and the dismal presence of diversity in top jobs is not necessarily to get rid of men or to reject *every* 'male' way of doing business (some, but not all). It's to actively find a balance between the masculine and the feminine in ourselves and in corporate culture. That is the only way any of us can truly 'have it all'.

Don't Be Afraid to Get Close

Reed Hastings, CEO of Netflix, famously described his workforce as a 'dream team... in which *all* of your colleagues are extraordinary at what they do and are highly effective collaborators'.[14] They model themselves 'on being a team, not a family', since a family gives unconditional love, despite a relative's bad behaviour after too many hot toddies at Christmas.

They love the sports metaphor at Netflix, saying the dream team works together 'in pursuit of ambitious common goals', comparing leaders to coaches and that *every* player on the field is amazing at their position, and plays very effectively with the others... A dream team is about pushing yourself to be the best teammate you can be, caring intensely about your teammates, and knowing that you may not be on the team forever.'

While I agree with Hastings about every player being amazing at their position and working collaboratively for the greater good, I prefer the family metaphor. It feels more com-passionate and less competitive. The bonds between people in an office are what hold it together, in lean and fat years. I always like our office to feel like a home away from home; colleagues really are like a family. You spend more time with the people at work than you do with your home family. Your fortunes rise and fall together, like a real familial unit. You live through so many life experiences together – marriages, kids, divorce, illness, death. So, of course, you should treat work family with as much love, support and respect as you do your nearest and dearest.

Members of our leadership team have been with us for sixteen, twelve, eleven, ten and eight years. These people and I have shared quite a lot of our lives together. Weddings have been shared, we've been there for the births of children and we've mourned together over the loss of loved ones. We cele-brate together. My colleagues have been to stay at my house for the weekend. Our lives have been enriched by each other. Our business has been enriched, too, by our mutual trust and reli-ance. John Frieda, my incredible friend and long-standing client, once told me that you should only do business with people you also want to hang out with, and I totally agree.

It seems obvious, and yet hardly any companies encourage close personal relationships. The default assumption among bosses and employees, or between same-level colleagues, is that caring too much dulls the competitive edge. I happen to believe that it sharpens it. If you truly love and care for your colleagues, you work that much harder for all of your sakes.

The office is not the Trump White House. You need not worry that at any moment a colleague is going to stab you in the back or in the front. If a workplace is as hostile as the Roman Senate, it will most likely destroy itself and everyone in it.

Most of us rely on the workplace to supply us with friends, often romantic partners, or even just to fulfil basic human social needs. Forming close, loving, affectionate relationships with the people you spend so much time with is only natural! It should be encouraged. I've found my best friends in life in the workplace. If it weren't for work, school and university, I wouldn't have any friends at all. I imagine that's true for many of us. As a boss, I try to go above and beyond. I really care for our staff. I welcome and enjoy the responsibility of caring for them with loving kindness, and to be involved in their lives.

As a leader it can be awkward to give negative feedback to a work-family member. But who better to deliver harsh truths than a trusted and close 'family' member? Who else will tell a slipping colleague what they really need to hear, even if it's painful for both the messenger and the recipient? As is often the case, what really matters most is not what one says, but how one says it. I do this privately, and always from a place of sincerity and genuine care. When the message is understood, the end result is normally gratitude from the appraisee in question. They feel that out of the public eye, their friend and colleague has done them a huge service of pulling them up (with compassion) and given them tools to help them improve. Nine times out of ten, they go on to succeed very effectively in their workplace, and the friendship becomes even more trusting and deep. The opposite of honesty is what you often find in BS offices that run on gossip – people talking behind each other's backs instead of addressing the offender to their face. This just wastes time and changes nothing.

I should mention that total honesty has, at times, worked against me. When I've had to share bad news about the company, people don't like it. In the movies, if there's a bad boss or a toxic workplace, employees are kept in the dark about what's really going on, and then learn they've all been fired. We try to keep everyone informed about all of our news – both good and bad – and it's possible that some people would rather not hear the truth. I have had some personality conflicts about this because I don't advocate ignorance, blissful or otherwise.

Encourage Ethical Workplace Relationships

At TCS, our staff force is over 80 per cent female, and we have never experienced harassment problems. What we have seen are some beautiful relationships that started here. A man who worked for one of our clients took up with a staffer from our beauty department, and I believe they are very happy. We've had two marriages between account execs and the journalists they got to know while pitching products. Once, a client fell head over heels for his account manager. Their working together became untenable, though, so the manager did the sensible thing and left TCS to take a new job elsewhere, let the client stay at TCS and continued the relationship.

Romances between employees and clients are not ideal, and I'm not in favour of that. But, then again, you really can't help who you fall in love with. Who am I to discourage passion wherever it blooms? As long as the relationship is not between an employee and someone higher up, a person who decides on their promotions and pay rises, I'm okay with it. It's really hard out there – there are so many things to do, like get a job, pay the rent, be fit, make and save money. One thing that can make it all manageable is a loving relationship. I am definitely not going to stop anybody from falling in love in the workplace because, to be honest, that's going to be the most likely place to meet people.

One very positive aspect of a more female culture in the workplace is that women do tend to nurture and care about relationships. It's one of those soft skills that might be thought of in the traditional business culture as a weakness. In a BS office, people don't talk about their families or friends as much, and visits from spouses and children are frowned upon. Indeed, having 'personal' issues at all is a chink in the armour. Often, employees at BS offices keep their illnesses and divorces a secret so they won't be seen as vulnerable by their colleagues.

From my perspective, the talent for personal interaction is one of the greatest strengths of TCS. As leaders, my partners and I are unequivocally in favour of our staff forming close, personal friendships and to be emotionally involved. We've had office mates become apartment mates and godparents to each other's kids. Staffers spend Christmases with one another. One of our employees came to London from the other side of the world, didn't know anyone and formed her entire friendship group at TCS. To this day, her best friends in the world came from our office. Our people build lifelong connections that nurture their souls while earning a decent living. Honestly, what could be a better reflection of our office culture? We need to separate emotional closeness and love from sexual harassment and abuse. They have nothing to do with each other. No one would disagree that a workplace with more closeness and love, and zero abuse, would be a nicer place to work. No place is a perfect utopia, of course. Some relationships can be prickly. You can only do your best to create the most comfortable space possible.

Take Caring Seriously

It takes so little effort to be involved. All you have to do is ask people about their lives with genuine interest, and they will share their hearts with you. You don't have to pry. Just say, 'Hello, how are you today?' That question is not pro forma. When I ask, I want an honest answer. I really want to *know*.

If the reply is, 'I'm not so great', go the next step and ask, 'What's wrong?' Maybe the dog is sick or they're having trouble sleeping. Maybe they're stressed out about their kid's university application process (been there!). Maybe their roof literally fell in. These home concerns matter at work. It's unrealistic to think that people's personal lives won't affect their professional performance. I'm not saying the office should be one big group therapy session. We don't send round a daily newsletter with our feelings updates. But we all have emotions and they need to be given some air. We are not robots; we can't be 100 per cent every day, because life inevitably gets in the way. So why don't we just acknowledge this and give people the support they need?

As human beings, we have good days and bad days. I'm sure many BS companies would rather their people behave like machines and demand robotic consistency. As a boss, it can be frustrating for an employee to have an off day when I really need them fired up. But if I were to react to a down cycle with pressure, demands, criticism and threats, it would only prolong it. Instead, when I see someone struggling, I find out what's going on. Then I can take steps to make things better and speed the return to happiness and high performance.

My jaw dropped when I read about US car maker Tesla's attendance policies for its factory workers in California.[15] Managers are allowed to punish workers who arrive one minute late to work or leave one minute early. If an employee shows up five minutes late five times, they can be fired. Workers who attempted to unionize to change these harsh rules were pushed out of the company. Somehow, Tesla called their policies 'fair' and 'just'. Really? They seem pretty unfair and unjust to me. What about making allowances for a mother caring for a sick child or a commuter getting stuck in traffic? Such strict rules ignore the realities of life and punish the very people Tesla should be rewarding and trusting to make their cars. And is it not ironic that Elon Musk got emotional in the *New York Times* about the pressures of his work/life imbalance, his inability to sleep, not seeing his children or family, running in and out of his brother's wedding and ill-considered tweets? What about giving hard-working employees the benefit of the doubt?

Recently, we had a difficult moment with a long-time client. A few things were not going as we had hoped, and I asked a senior account person to go to an event we were running, make herself highly visible and apologize for a misunderstanding. She promised she'd be there to smooth any ruffled feathers. I could not get there myself and I knew she would stabilize the relationship perfectly. As it happened, my plans changed, and I decided at the last minute to go to the event to support her and was surprised that she was not there. At a BS office, I'm sure the boss would have sent her some angry 'Where the hell are you?' texts that demonstrated a basic lack of trust.

I knew her to be responsible and passionate about her work. I also know a great deal about her as a human being. If she wasn't where she was supposed to be, something was wrong. I reacted intuitively like a concerned friend or mum, and sent her an email, asking, 'Are you okay?' It turned out that she had fallen, hurt her back and had to go to the hospital. Imagine if I'd come down hard on her for missing an event while she was in agony at A & E!

In an office culture of distrust, if a colleague starts missing deadlines and not performing, her colleagues and bosses are most likely in the dark about what's really going on and also discouraged from finding out. So, in the absence of compassion, one co-worker's inefficiency might cause others to harbour resentment and spread negativity about her to others, compounding difficulties all around and distracting everyone from their own work. Everyone suffers.

In a no-BS office with a trusting culture, colleagues ask the troubled team member, 'What's the matter?' She would feel safe to share her story about what's upsetting her. As caring, sympathetic humans, co-workers would rally around her and pick up the reins on the project to allow her the space and time to recover. She'd heal more quickly with the support and would spread gratitude and positivity to others in the team. Everyone is happy.

What goes around comes around. Ideally, we would never have to face personal devastation in our lives. But, I'm sorry to say, the odds are that, at some point, you will. The person who got some slack during a rough patch will *run* to her co-worker's side to help her through her own difficulties. People helping people; companies helping people; people helping companies – this is the wheel of compassion and friendship I would be happy to be caught up in.

Culture is the context in which people live and work. If they do so in a culture of comfort, compassion, closeness and trust, it stands to reason that they will feel positive about being there and aspire in their passion and productivity to stay there. Sharing everything – feelings, glory, hard times, failures, the load, our lives – doubles the joy and halves the pain of whatever life brings. Being part of a no-BS office like this does not feel like work. It feels like an extraordinary privilege.

CULTURE

A healthy office culture feels like being part of a club of which anyone would want to be a member. Here are some of the ways in which we uphold our culture and values:

- Collaboration brings out the best in team members to inspire and support each other.
- Prevent interpersonal or work problems by talking about what's going on and finding solutions as a group.
- Every. Single. Person in the room should feel safe enough to speak up and contribute to the discussion.
- When you trust each other, creativity and compassion flows.
- It's okay to make friends at work!
- Allow people to be human. They have problems and emotions and need to be given some air. If you know what's going on with an individual, you'll rally around to help. And they'll do the same for you one day.

3 Communication

One day during one of my early *Devil Wears Prada* jobs, my boss marched me from the office to a 'meeting'. I was told to make sure I had a piece of paper and a pencil, nothing more. We were actually headed to my boss's hair appointment at a very upscale salon in Mayfair owned by one of her top clients. The salon was the most gorgeous place where royalty, aristocrats and London's A-listers went for the UK's best hair-dressing services. While my boss was having her hair done, she rattled off notes for me to write down. I stood next to her, scribbling on a notepad. She said, 'You're in the way. Sit *down*.' I looked around for a chair to grab. She rolled her eyes and said, 'On the *floor*.'

I hesitated, but only for a second, and then lowered myself to the floor of the salon and took dictation while she shouted over the hairdryer. A few minutes later, the door opened and the owner himself walked in. He came directly over and said to my boss, 'Hello, how are you? Why is this girl on the floor? If it's okay with you, in my salon, people sit on chairs.' And he dragged one over for me.

If the floor could have opened and swallowed me up, I would have been grateful. I was mortified! It was a huge moment for me. Here was a clear distinction between one boss who sent the message loud and clear that she didn't care about people's feelings, and another who went out of his way to make others feel respected.

That incident made a deep impression on me. I realized that people communicate who they are in everything they say and do, and that the message one sends, in both words and actions, has consequences. If someone is imperious and rude, no-BS people won't want to work with them. In fact, soon after that encounter, the client cut ties with my boss. It was probably just one too many uncomfortable, awkward incidents for him to take before he said enough is enough.

My job is to sell communications, literally. But the truth is, we're all the CEOs of our own individual 'communications store' where the only product we are selling is ourselves. By communications, I don't mean just verbal, non-verbal and written correspondence. It goes deeper than that. Everything you say and do communicates who you are, and what you have to offer. Ideally, you will communicate your values, confidence, strong work ethic and kindness to clients, colleagues and bosses, and they will respond with respect and appreciation. Good interpersonal skills build and strengthen relationships. Communications breakdowns – all the rude, hostile, passive-aggressive, dishonest ways people interact with each other – are just bad business. They hamper relationships and negatively impact creativity and productivity.

Make Sure They Know You Care

My communications style is rooted in compassion. What and how I express myself will make an impact on whoever I'm speaking to, and I'd like it to be net positive for both of us. If I'm kind, that kindness will be repaid. Princess Diana was very much a supporter of this life philosophy. 'Carry out a random act of kindness, with no expectation of reward, safe in the knowledge that one day someone might do the same for you,' she once said.[1]

I was reminded of that quote at work when I was walking up the stairs and saw a young woman, a new intern, coming up. I hadn't had a welcome breakfast with her yet to break the ice, and when she saw me, she looked away nervously. I flashed back to being new, and young, and immediately empathized with her self-consciousness.

I said, 'Hey, how are you? I'm very sorry, but I don't know your name yet. I'm Julietta. It's nice to meet you.'

She seemed embarrassed and said, 'I'm just the intern. Molly.'

'How long have you been here, Molly?' I asked. 'What side of the business are you working in? And, by the way, "just the intern" is not going to work for me – you're a potential CEO of tomorrow.'

We chatted until she seemed to relax, and then we went our separate ways, both of us feeling better for that brief exchange. I pray people will show similar kindness to my daughters as they enter the workforce, because I know and can remember how terrifying it can be to start out.

Kindness can buoy the spirit and is its own reward. But it can have unexpected positive consequences, too. Hours after that interaction on the stairs, I got an email that said, 'I heard you met my daughter Molly on the stairs today and took the time to talk to her. It just made her day. Starting out is always so hard, and you stopping to chat really made a difference. Thank you.'

By the way, that woman, Molly's mother? She happened to be Fiona Golfar, editor-at-large of British *Vogue*. I'd no idea that her daughter was interning with us. By empathizing with the intern and taking the time to chat for no more than two minutes, I helped her. I don't doubt she will go on to be a superstar.

NICENESS GOES A LONG WAY

Not to belabour the staircase example, but the fact is the people you meet on the way up in your career are the same ones you will meet on the way down. If you are rude and dismissive when you are on top, don't expect to be treated with compassion when you've fallen off your perch.

Being kind can transform an office from a place of fear to a haven of freedom. It's just a matter of asking, 'Would you like a cup of tea?' or 'Can I help you with that?' Hold the lift doors. Grab a sandwich for a swamped office mate. Remember birthdays.

Compassion costs you nothing, with such high returns! Your wealth is your reputation. Every act of kindness is bankable. It goes right into your account, and that wealth will be there for you when you need it. And likewise, it sounds harsh, but screw up once, be horrible to a colleague just once, and they tend to never forget it – unless you apologize!

Mind Your Manners

Steve Jobs, visionary founder of Apple, was known for his vision and passion – and his rudeness. In Walter Isaacson's biography *Steve Jobs*, he recounted examples of the icon's impolite behaviour: repeatedly cursing at colleagues, asking an interviewee if he was a virgin, yelling at smoothie makers at Whole Foods, firing people without warning or in front of a room full of people telling business partners, 'Everything you've ever done in your life is shit' and 'You don't know what you're doing', and yelling at hotel clerks. Isaacson asked one of Jobs' friends, Jony Ive, why the man was so rude. His response: 'When [Jobs is] very frustrated... his way to achieve catharsis is to hurt somebody. And I think he feels he has a liberty and license to do that. The normal rules of social engagement, he feels, don't apply to him.'[2]

Maybe Steve Jobs could get away with it. For the rest of us, part of building trusting relationships is having high standards of behaviour for yourself. If you are abrupt and caustic, people won't be as open to friendship with you. Our staff is expected to say 'Hello', 'Goodbye', 'Please', 'I'm sorry', 'Thank you' and 'Great job!' to one another and we listen without interruption while others speak. It drives me crazy when people talk over one another, thinking the loudest voice in the room will hold sway. Besides the fact that they're wrong (the best thing to do is to be totally silent in a meeting and, instantly, people will wonder 'What's he thinking?' and want to know), interrupting is just rude.

When clients arrive at the office, the receptionist – in my opinion, the most important ambassador for the company

– takes their coat, shows them to the loo and offers them something to drink, within two minutes of arrival. If clients need a few minutes to collect their thoughts, we clear a room. When they walk into a meeting, we all stand up. If we're taking clients to lunch, they choose the location and we make the reservation. They pick which seat they'd like at the table first. When they leave, someone accompanies them to the door, waits with them at the lift and helps them with their bags. I hear that journalists breathe a sigh of relief when they realise that TCS is 'front of house' at the international roster of Fashion Weeks. They know they will be looked after and that we will genuinely do our best.

I can't tell you the number of times I've heard, 'Julietta, TCS people are so polite.' Have we won clients because of our good manners? Maybe. People are eager to do business with us because we are pleasant to be around.

Just Tell the Truth

There are a handful of ways people lie at work. An office-politics player might lie about a colleague's input to make himself look better. A gossip might spread lies to make herself feel and seem more 'plugged in' than she actually is. An insecure worker might falsely blame someone else for making his mistake in order to protect himself. People might 'pad' their CV or inflate their salaries when interviewing for a new job. They might claim to have a cold when they call in sick but are really just hungover.

Every lie told has a cumulative effect. A little white lie might seem harmless, but over time someone who repeatedly sells untruths will earn their reputation, and all they will communicate to others is untrustworthiness.

An effective communicator expresses their – and their company's and client's – perspective with transparency and integrity. This means telling the truth. Regardless of their stock-in-trade – be it a widget, their expertise or labour – their job is to convince others to buy it or believe them. Without a ring of truth in one's communications, how would anyone make a sale?

Often in a traditional, short-term-profit-only business, the truth is thrown out of the window or skirted with an 'I didn't know.' Good liars are seen as assets. But you don't build long-term clients and customers by selling BS.

One of my pre-TCS bosses instructed me to tell a client that we were raising our fee by 30 per cent because we'd been doing more for him than his old fee justified. The truth was, he was paying a fair amount and we weren't going to do anything to justify charging him more. The internal reason for raising his fee was that the company at large wasn't hitting its numbers for the quarter, and this ruse would help to fix that. I was being asked to lie to a client I'd spent two years working with closely, a man I liked, who'd been kind to me and trusted me. I knew that he was spending as much as he could on publicity already and that increasing his fee might not be possible for his business.

'It doesn't seem right to...' I protested to the boss.

'This isn't a discussion,' she replied. 'If you can't do this, you're obviously not commercial, and not very good at your job.'

My choices were to either lose my integrity or my job. I decided to keep my integrity and left the agency.

There was no way I could knowingly lie to anyone, let alone a client I'd had a great relationship with. When I called him to say I was leaving the company and that his account would be handled by someone else, I thanked him for being such a pleasure to work with. I added one more item to the ever-growing list of things I would do differently when, if, I ever started my own company.

The new account person spoke to my former client about the change in his charges. Apparently, he was a bit shaken by my leaving and decided that he needed some continuity, so he agreed to stay with the agency and pay the higher fee. However, after two months of no added value from the agency, he realized he'd been swindled and took his business elsewhere.

If the agency hadn't inflated his fee, he would have continued to be a client in good standing for many months, maybe years, to come and would have contributed far more money to the agency's bottom line that year. (And perhaps I might have stayed at the agency.) Not only did the client withdraw his business, he might have told others about his experience, and advised them not to sign on or stay with the agency. To me, this is the worst type of short-termism. I know that some people get away with it for a long time – they may be financially richer, but they are ethically and morally bankrupt. I'd rather make a bit less money and still be able to look at myself in the mirror every morning.

I don't mean to imply that I walk around with a halo over my head. I've convinced clients to make choices that turned out to be ill-advised. I've made mistakes, big ones. But I've never intentionally lied to anyone to fatten my wallet or protect my own skin. When I mess up, I own it, and then I set out to correct it.

As I've told my daughters since they were little, 'Everyone makes mistakes. What you do next defines the difference.'

Honesty can have its vulnerabilities

Talented posers can con people into believing they are what they appear to be. A few times over the years, I've hired real masters at this game and been burned badly. After their true selves were shown and they left the company, I rushed to blame myself for not seeing through the disguise. But if I were to be less trusting, then I wouldn't be true to my nature. After one quite staggering betrayal, I spent considerable time soul-searching and questioning my ability to be a good judge of character and, frankly, a reliable leader. The experience knocked my confidence, my fundamental belief in myself and my capabilities. If I could get someone *so* wrong, then what's not to say I won't make the same mistake all over again?

Some people don't trust anyone until they've proven themselves worthy. Others trust everyone until they prove themselves unworthy. I am the latter. In the weeks after that messy situation when I trusted too easily and paid the price for that mistake, I thought hard about trying to change my personality. Should I adopt a 'prove yourself or you're invisible' methodology? Well, I couldn't even if I wanted to. I choose to have faith in human beings. There will always be the boyfriend, the family member, the colleague who disappoints, sometimes monstrously. But most people will live up to our faith in them.

One of TCS's most extraordinary and long-term clients was ESPA Skincare founder, Sue Harmsworth. Sue is extremely successful and someone I admire so much. Having sold her company in 2018, she is living her best life. At a lunch in London she told me that, in her entire career, two or three people had betrayed her really badly. One of them called her recently to ask if she'd like a coffee, to let bygones be bygones. Her reply was a firm, relaxed but self-assured, 'No'. Sue had created so many precious, powerful relationships and life-long friendships throughout her working life, why on earth would she need to spend any time at all with someone who had let her down so horribly? Life is too short for liars.

Under-promise and Over-deliver

In business, there is a huge temptation to use bluster and exaggeration. Some people really do believe that they have to lie and inflate to get ahead. One famous devotee of this school of thought is none other than American president, Donald Trump, who once wrote, 'A little hyperbole never hurts. People want to believe that something is the biggest and the greatest and the most spectacular. I call it truthful hyperbole. It's an innocent form of exaggeration – and a very effective form of promotion.'[3]

'Truthful hyperbole' is not innocent in any way if the intention is to deceive. Actually, fraud is never 'innocent'. It's putting profit over honesty as a basic business principle. But using 'hyperbole' to fool people will only work for so long.

When someone oversells herself – her accomplishments or what a client can expect from her going forward – she puts herself on the back foot from the outset. Unless she can pull off every outrageous claim, her client will inevitably be disappointed. It's not strategic to promise the moon and stars. An unexpected crisis might pop up and, no matter what excuses she makes to the client, they'll be underwhelmed. They expected a lot more *because that's what she told them.*

Our strategy is to communicate the opposite of bluster, though at the same time we don't aim half-cock; we truly dream for the very best, but try to manage the realities of what can get in the way (and the truth is, things don't often go to plan). We always try hard to under-promise and over-deliver, aka we 'manage expectations'. This strategy comes up often in politics. Before a big debate, for example, both sides will pump up the other candidate's skills and experience while downplaying their own. Some spin doctors will say that their candidate 'didn't even prepare'. The lower the bar, the more impressed the audience will be when a candidate crosses it. He'll come off like a superstar just by forming complete sentences.

In business, one should present as articulate and well-prepared at all times, of course. However, when we outline to a client what they can expect for, say, a launch event, we intentionally set realistic expectations. That way, when we exceed them, the client will be thrilled and see us as wizards. If we set high expectations, the client would only be embarrassed and disappointed unless we met them.

It's tragic in any business context to promise a five-star dinner and deliver a brown bag lunch. In 2017, Fyre Media Inc. CEO Billy McFarland and rapper Ja Rule announced via Instagram that they were organizing a luxury music festival on a private Bahaman island. Their marketing of the Fyre Festival was pure social media gold: for a promotional video to announce the event, they hired top influencers – models and actresses including Kendall Jenner, Bella Hadid and Emily Ratajkowski – to pose in bikinis on speed boats, on a beach and other exotic locations, and then asked them to post about this festival to end all festivals on their Twitter and Instagram accounts. Customers snapped up expensive packages that included gourmet food and drink, luxury villas and prime seating for all the A-list concerts. The event sold out quickly and looked like it'd be a huge success.

Meanwhile, back on the island, organizers and their employees faced obstacle after obstacle as a result of gross mismanagement and incompetence. The luxury villas turned out to be flimsy tents. The gourmet meals were cold sandwiches. The location had no mobile phone service or running water or sufficient bathrooms. Every music act that had been originally booked for the festival cancelled when they learned the organizers hadn't constructed an adequate stage. Guests arrived, and were shocked by what they found, compared to what they'd paid for. In the end, investors and contractors lost millions. Workers never received their salaries, and some lost money they'd loaned to McFarland. The event was an unmitigated disaster. Due to poor organization and bad planning, guests were stuck on the island without facilities, food, water or adequate housing. Their desperation turned the scene into a *Lord of the Flies* or *Hunger Games* situation.[4] McFarland was hit with eight lawsuits, and ultimately pleaded guilty to wire fraud and was ordered to forfeit $26 million.

If McFarland had listened to the warnings from his staff who told him they didn't have the time, money or location to deliver on what he'd promised, cancelled the event and returned customers' money, he might not be serving a six-year sentence in prison in New York State today.

DO THE RIGHT THING

If you have been in a traditional office culture for a few years, you have probably been asked to exaggerate or obfuscate by now. It might have been a small embellishment or an outright, unconscionable lie. People often choose to shelve their reservations about intentional deception and just go along with it to gain favour with the boss, calling it a compromise (and ignoring 'the knowing' in their belly). BS bosses would have you lose your moral compass to make a short-term gain. Unfortunately, your 'spinning' for a living won't reward you directly. You'll end up enriching people 'higher up' the food chain in exchange for sacrificing your morals, for the chance to lie again on a bigger stage or in a more senior role one day. It hardly seems like a worthy goal for any ethical, honest person.

As an alternative, practise honesty as a matter of course. That might mean re-evaluating your chosen profession and pursuing a career in a field that doesn't require spinning or fudging. It might be difficult at times to be so relentlessly honest; people might prefer a pretty lie to the unvarnished truth, but if the message is delivered with care, and is meant to help not hurt, you are doing the right thing and will sleep well at night.

What You See Is What You Get

If you are to communicate one trait above all others, let it be authenticity. People 'read' realness instinctively and are naturally suspicious of anyone who comes off as phony. In many contexts in our society, 'fake' is the very worst thing one can be. The reason people assume a set of values and behaviours that don't reflect their true self, is to appear 'tough' or even follow what they perceive to be the corporate culture in their workplace – they are trying to survive or, better, succeed. This often works in the short-term, but after a while it starts to grate, because it is not who they really are. Authenticity is communicated through word choice, tone of voice, eye contact, appearance, behaviour... the list goes on. If a person tries to project an image that conflicts with their true self, people will sense the disconnect in a heartbeat.

And as trite as it may seem, actions do speak louder than words. Quite often, people say the right things, but then go and do something contradictory. Either way, saying one thing and doing another reads as inauthentic and therefore suspicious.

The simple solution is to be oneself, relentlessly. Of course, in a corporate setting, one should be more professional in manner and dress than when hanging out with old friends at the pub. The idea is to be the same person with a workplace-appropriate demeanour. Being a completely different person at work and at home might be possible, but it's not emotionally sustainable for most people. It will be draining to put on an act all day long.

People are complex, of course. We all have many sides to our personalities, but it's important to be the same complicated, multifaceted person at home and at work, instead of showing only one face in one place. Being one-faced is just as disingenuous as being two-faced. To be genuine and authentic, share your whole self (on your best behaviour) with others.

I'm pretty sure I'm just as complicated as anyone else, but being true to myself prevails wherever I am. I have the same values and personality whether I'm giving an ad hoc tutorial in the office or cooking for my family in the kitchen.

DON'T BLAG IT

When you have any opportunity to communicate who you are and what you can do with a client or leader, take it. Deliver a detailed description of the work you have painstakingly laboured over. Share what you've learned, reveal your passion with an enthusiastic response and show your strength and vulnerability by telling the truth, by not being afraid to express yourself – even if it's bad news. That said, don't gush and go on too long, either. Be precise *and* concise. Carefully consider every word, and make sure it needs to be said before taking up people's time with it.

Communicate a Unique Perspective

Authenticity by another name is non-suggestibility, or not blindly going along. Often nobody bothers to ask, 'Do I *really* want to be on Twitter? What are the consequences? Is it good for me?' Being non-suggestible is having the personal strength and passion of one's convictions to think, 'Just because everyone is doing a thing doesn't mean I have to do it, too.'

Stop for a minute and ask, 'Just because x product is always pitched the same way, does that mean I have to do it that way, too?' It is essential to question conventional 'wisdom' and form one's own opinion instead. As a boss, I'm searching for and rewarding people who have fresh insight and new ideas. No business in the modern world can survive by just relying on what's been successful in the past. We need thoughtful, considered people who are brave enough to buck popular opinion. *Un*conventional wisdom moves the needle.

Another way to be non-suggestible is to rely on the values of passion and honesty. Ask, 'What do I really love?' and 'What really gets me excited (even if it's a bit embarrassing)?' I once gave an interview about what I did to ward off the stress of being a CEO. I think the reporter wanted me to say I had a shiatsu therapist, a great yoga instructor or a favourite mineral bath product. Instead, I said, 'I do needlepoint.'

She said, 'What?' and looked at me like I must be joking and laughed out loud. 'Are you sure you want to say that in public?'

She'd made other assumptions, clearly. There I was, in her mind I guess, a fashion and beauty PR doyenne, with access to all kinds of luxury goods and services, and I said that I unwind by doing needlework like an old lady hunched over her hoop. I admit, it *is* an amusing sight and has earned me a few double takes in airport lounges over the years, but being authentic is more important than appearing 'cool'.

I was so motivated by the reporter's astonished reaction that I sent a company-wide email that said, 'Hey guys, as many of you know, I enjoy tapestry to keep myself stress- and anxiety-free. If anybody wants to learn how to do it, I'll get some needles here and will teach you.' Everybody at the office laughed about it. Some took to calling me Granny. And I loved it. I thought, *Good! Let them see that the rules of cool don't apply here.* If I'm not ashamed or scared to tell people that I love my needles and embroidery thread, then they won't be intimidated to break out of the tribe mentality and will share their 'weird' pastimes as well.

Being non-suggestible and unafraid to reveal one's true self takes real courage and strength, full stop. Being true to who you are is key, in both life and work. By not just following the herd, an authentic person can bring new, fresh ideas to the office that could make all the difference. Every company needs original thinkers, and no-BS bosses really value them.

Deliver a Consistent Message

When a boss or colleague's behaviour is inconsistent – one day, they're nice; the next, they're horrible – people feel anxious. A frightened staff member is not a productive one. Anyone who co-parents knows how important consistency is. Both parents have to be on the same page or the child will feel insecure and anxious, which can lead to emotional issues later on.

It's essential that our staff gets a consistent message from me about what I expect, what I'd like them to do and what I'll do. Since I expect them to work very hard, the least I can do as a leader is to be predictable in this sense. Although our work flow might change from week to week, our leadership style and core values won't. It's the same with clients. I'm consistent in my communications with them so they know who they're talking to and that they can rely on me to be the same person the day we met, and ten years from now. Strong relationships might start with a respectful first impression, but that's not worth much if it isn't followed through in the second, third or fourth meeting. After proving oneself to be reliable and consistent, a good start can develop into a relationship that is steady, strong and mutually beneficial. I don't put on my best behaviour to lure in a client and then show a different set of colours once the ink is dry on the contract. I might not be as good an actress as other PR professionals. Fortunately, if someone has self-awareness, values and can deliver on their promises, they don't need drama.

Choose Your Words with Care and Wisdom

After addressing the big areas of ethical and compassionate communications style – honesty, authenticity and non-suggestibility – comes the practical specifics. The first line of effective communication is language. Word choice might be the difference between a green light and a full stop. No matter what, precise, thoughtful language is the goal; mumbles and vague platitudes only communicate uselessness and confusion.

Once, years ago, I sent a junior exec to a John Frieda editorial photo shoot. When John called, in his usual meticulous way, to ask how it went, the account exec said, 'It was fine, yeah, it was all fine.' I got a call from John a little later that day, and he was not happy. 'It was *fine* darling!' was not what he wanted to hear. Firstly, he was not confident that this exec knew what good, or fine, or exceptional looked like on a shoot. He wanted to hear that the lighting was flawless, that the model's hair responded well to the product, that the make-up did not overshadow the hair, and so on. Light, glib, ill-considered words spoken without thought or depth are most often received as they are delivered!

It's only too easy, without clarity, for messages to be misunderstood. Back in 1997, Tom and I were lucky enough to win the account of the organic, all-natural skincare brand Dr. Hauschka. We wanted to deliver a four- or five-page feature on the company in one of the very top publications. *Vogue* was an obvious first choice, so I pitched to Kathy Phillips, then the revered health and beauty director. She had a reputation for being a hard taskmaster and knew her stuff thousands of times better than I did. I was terrified to reach out to her.

I managed to get an appointment with her and her assistant. I knew that Kathy was passionate about natural beauty and had a genuine and personal interest in it. To that end, I knew she would 'get it', and be totally in love with this extraordinary brand. It was right up her street. We met at a Mayfair hotel in London. I felt like it was a huge moment in my career, finally meeting this industry icon. I'd rehearsed my pitch for days and nights. I could do it in two minutes if that's all she'd give me. We had a wonderful meeting. I was given ample time to pitch, and I felt reasonably confident that she'd heard me.

The following week I called Kathy's office to see if she was interested, but I didn't hear back. The week after, no call. The week after that... still nothing. I followed up as much as I could before it felt stalker-y, and then Tom and I decided we'd have to move on. I pitched to Newby Hands, the then-beauty director of *Harper's Bazaar*. Newby, also an industry icon, listened to me carefully. The problem was that natural beauty was not Newby's passion point. She was much more interested in the latest science and technology emerging in the industry. But, to my total shock, she got it and came with me to those rose fields at WALA, the foundation behind the Dr. Hauschka skincare company. She wrote the most beautiful, incredible feature which quite literally carried the brand and was its foundational driver in the UK.

When the feature was published, Tom and I were beyond thrilled, as was our client, Sebastian Parsons. The day after its publication, Kathy Phillips called me and asked why I had not pitched the story to her. I nearly fell off my chair.

I thought about what happened and realized that I must not have projected. I hadn't made myself clear, and she didn't register my well-rehearsed, probably terrified pitch as a pitch. She remembered the tea appointment well, but somehow I had not gotten through to her about the client. Kathy has become a friend and is also a client of TCS with her brand, This Works. We laugh together about our sometimes failure to communicate well. I might say to her, 'KP, I don't want this to be another Dr. H moment... '

Even with the best intentions, sometimes the message is muddled. It's always wise to consider the difference between what is being said and what is heard.

It seems like every good language communication word starts with a C: clarity, cleverness, considerate, considered. In a meeting, I would put clarity over cleverness any day. It's one thing to be witty, but if the client fails to understand the point or, God forbid, doesn't get the punchline, the joke isn't so funny anymore.

WATCH YOUR LANGUAGE!

I understand that swearing can provide an elegant emphasis, and I am all for precision and clarity. For some people, though, it is just vulgar. In England, the culture is to swear quite a lot, but it's not the same in the US and many other countries we do business with. There have been incidents when a member of staff cursed on the phone with foreign clients and offended them terribly.

In my personal conversations, I'm comfortable with swearing. But I really try not to use the F-word at work. It's impossible to know how a client or colleague will react, so it doesn't seem worth the risk of offending them. Even if the situation couldn't be more f***ed-up, I dig into my vocabulary to find another – clean – way to express those feelings.

Ask the Right Question

An amazing tactic we've learned from Liz Villani – founder of Courageous Success, a brilliant leadership, coaching and values consultancy – is always to start a question with 'what' rather than 'why'. 'What' is objective, whereas 'why' is judgemental.

This one-word choice makes a big difference in allowing for an open conversation to challenge the work on the table. 'What was the reason you decided on that tack?' starts a dialogue, whereas 'Why did you do that?' sounds critical and accusatory. And then the person who is in the hot seat will become defensive.

I will go to any lengths to avoid backing someone into a corner and making them feel like they have to fight their way out. When someone becomes defensive, it's embarrassing for everyone at the table. Any deflection sounds to my ears like a weak justification or an 'It wasn't my fault', and usually turns into them trying to blame others. The blame game is a BS business standard. I much, much prefer it when someone asks to speak to me privately and says, 'Listen, there is a problem. I've made a mistake.' In this case, two things need to happen. The first is that precious time is not wasted working out what happened – the 'who did what' and 'where' the problem originated. The second is that we move on quickly to fix it. Often, this time is critical to keeping the client or making amends.

Actively Listen

Liz has also taught me that there are four ways that humans listen to each other.

The first way – which accounts for the vast majority of listening – is when someone else is talking, and one's mind drifts to thoughts that have nothing to do with the discussion, such as, 'I wonder what's for supper?', 'Looks like rain' or 'When can I get out of here already?' Although many of us are skilled multitaskers, it's simply not possible to think two different things at the same time. Even a fleeting thought is an interruption that takes away from the conversation at hand. I have sat across from people countless times who nodded and smiled at all the right moments, but who I knew weren't really paying attention. No matter how skilled they might be at pretending to listen, I know intuitively that they're not fully present. It's disconcerting, and sometimes insulting. Above all, it sends the message, 'Whatever you are talking about is not that important to me right now.'

The second way of listening is hearing what someone is saying, but only relating it to oneself. An example would be meeting a friend for a drink after work. She says, 'I had the worst day! My boss is a nightmare. She kept me at work for twelve hours straight.' And then replying, 'That happened to me, too, but my boss is so much worse!' It's being on-topic, but off-subject, veering from 'you' to 'me'.

Understandably, we all need to express ourselves; to a degree, bringing up one's own comparable experience is how people commiserate. But a good listener would allow her friend to vent, paying her the service of being heard and validating her feelings. She'd show empathy, as in, 'I'm so sorry to hear that. You poor thing.' A bad listener hijacks the conversation from her friend to do her own venting or jumps in to offer unhelpful advice, which is just another way to assert one's own story above that of the other and bring one's ego to the top of the list. In effect, a hijacking 'listener' or unsolicited advice-giver is only serving herself. Most people find huge relief in just having someone take the time to listen.

The third way is not listening at all, when people block out anything they don't want to hear. It can be frustrating as a leader to try to give an employee my reaction to something, and to know that their defences have gone up, rendering them selectively deaf. None of us are in the business of wasting our breath or our time. I certainly don't need to listen to myself talk! It's essential to be able to open one's ears to feedback. When I receive criticism from my staff, I aim to listen honestly and constructively to what they have to say. If people can open their minds (and quiet their egos) to the possibility that they have much to gain from receiving feedback, they will go very far and so will their business. It's not required that people *agree* with the feedback they receive, but they must be open to the possibility that someone else might have thoughts worth listening to.

The final way of listening, which is extremely rare, is when the listener eyeballs the person she's talking to and really pays attention to what they're saying without allowing stray thoughts or ego to intrude. Believe me, it sounds easy, but it is so hard to do. It requires the listener to bite his lip when his own stories pop into his head, and to stay tuned in while the other person goes on. It's worth it, though. The speaker will intuitively know the listener is present and that for a few minutes someone really heard them. I am no psychologist, but I know from personal experience that when I've had a problem and I've had the blessing of a friend or colleague who just listens, it helps so much.

When I talk about active listening, people often say, 'That's exactly what I do *all the time.*' It's certainly what we'd like to think we do. But blocking one's own thoughts is not so easy. We all have our own problems, distractions and deadlines, and it can seem excruciating to slow down and take the time to focus on someone else's. It's like the Commandment, 'Do unto others...' Piece of cake, right? It's not so easy to treat others with kindness, care and respect, all day long, every day, but, if people can manage to do it, they are serving every person they meet well.

At TCS, we practise active listening at every meeting or discussion. I challenge the staff to pay attention not only to whoever is speaking, but also to be conscious about how well they listen and what is preventing them from doing it with both ears open. Not only is it polite – and, as you've seen, we care a lot about manners at TCS – but zoning out when someone is speaking blocks communication at the most basic level. It's funny how some people like the sound of their own voice better than any other.

Hurry to Deliver Bad News

One of the trickiest communications skills I've had to master is delivering bad news to a client. For starters, it must be done gently, and quickly. However dire the situation, it is likely to be ten times worse if the client hears about it from someone else first. One of my earliest clients was a famous jeweller. Possibly one of the most famous of his era, he came to London from Switzerland to curate an important retrospective of his life's work. To put on the exquisite exhibition, he worked incredibly hard for weeks. I arranged for a reporter from a large newspaper to cover the opening. She wrote a fabulous story about the

Italian jeweller, but she confused his name with that of *another important* Italian jewellery house. It was a simple but enormous mistake. Weeks of work, a great deal of money spent getting the pieces together, insured properly and displayed beautifully, and the credit went to someone else.

While I was figuring out how to break the news to my client, he went out for dinner with a friendly competitor of his who brought the newspaper to show him the article. The client called me that night and said, 'If you had just picked up the phone and told me what had happened, I wouldn't have had to endure the embarrassment of being told by a rival.'

It was a bad day. As soon as I found out about the wrong name in the article that afternoon, I should have gone to see him, not just picked up the phone or sent an email, but taken a cab to his house. He deserved the courtesy of a face-to-face. I should have done it immediately. What made me hesitate was fear about how he'd react, and my own shame and embarrassment for not triple-checking all the facts in the story with the writer before it went to print. If only I'd done the right thing, I could have apologized properly and promised to make it up to him by getting him an even better placement next time, but, not surprisingly, there was no next time with that client.

For bad news, mistakes or misunderstandings of any kind at work, the one essential ingredient is sincerity. Don't bother with insincere 'sorry not sorry' apologies like, 'I'm sorry you are upset' or 'I'm sorry you misinterpreted my meaning.' We can all do each other a favour by being humble, admitting to being a cause, however small, of tension or issues, and then moving quickly to repair the problem. Anything else is a waste of time.

When a client is unhappy, it's usually because of one of two reasons: an execution problem or a communications breakdown. In the jeweller story, we had both problems. Execution problems are the lesser of the two evils. If someone at TCS has not done their job with the necessary passion and dedication and is incapable or unwilling to correct the mistakes, they will be removed from that account (or in rare, particularly egregious cases, the company). If they have done their job well but failed to communicate with confidence, I encourage and support them by doing all I can to coach them to overcome insecurity and vulnerability.

In nearly any context of communications, it is always best to get on with it. Do not prevaricate before getting to the difficult truth or point. You can end up saying something like, 'Listen, this is going to be a very difficult conversation. I don't want to delay or draw this out unnecessarily. I regret very much having to tell you x or y.' If you swerve around the issue for too long, this is more painful for the receiver. They know something bad is coming, they know you are awkward about it but they are still none the wiser. It is far kinder to have the courage to briefly set the scene (which gives them a moment to prepare themselves) and then deliver the news clearly and succinctly. Once you've done this, use your empathy and help the person by sharing their emotion or putting yourself in their shoes.

Defensiveness is the worst way to react, and will surely make the recipient of bad news even more upset. There's really no way to know how someone will react, but it's wise to expect a full range of negative emotions, such as annoyance, disappointment, anger, fear or panic. Instead of trying to change their feelings, validate them: 'I know how incredibly hard this is for you,' you could say. 'Is there anything I can do to help you now? Would you like a few minutes to be alone? Can I get you some coffee?' No-BS communicators use emotional intelligence to allow people to feel whatever it is they need to feel. And once they take a moment to calm down, the meeting can continue productively.

Say It Like You See It

If a client, boss or colleague asks for an honest opinion and if that opinion happens to be negative, it can be tricky to give it. On the one hand, one serves a client (and colleagues) by guarding, nurturing and protecting them. On the other hand, occasionally, to serve well, one must hurt feelings by telling a client (or colleague) that their products or ideas aren't so good. At TCS, we call this delicate discussion 'calling out the white elephant in the room'. Everyone is thinking it; good communicators have the guts to say it. Those who can are serving the client in the truest sense.

I remember very early on, right at the beginning of TCS, Tom and I had a new client, an accessories designer, who was putting out her second or third collection. We went to see it, and we just knew there and then that the market was in a different place. Editors were looking for a different style, and this was not ever going to be the 'look of the season'. The collection was just so wrong for the time – wrong fabric, wrong print, wrong everything. We both knew there was no way we could have gone to an editor with those belts, bags and hats.

Tom, ever the brilliant diplomat, gave it to her straight. He said, 'I'm afraid to tell you that we cannot promote this collection.' It was very hard for him to speak the words, not least because the designer could have decided to get rid of us on the spot. We knew she'd worked night after night designing it, and we still told her, 'This is not going to fly.' Tom and I just stood there while we waited for her reaction.

She was actually incredibly grateful for Tom's honesty. She trusted his judgement and quickly moved on to building one of the most successful print-based businesses in the UK.

No-BS businesspeople appreciate honesty, as hard as it is to hear. They're self-aware enough to know that not all new products are going to be fantastic. And that's okay! An innovative company is going to take a few wrong turns. Google bombed with its wearable tech Google Glass, but it survived to launch Google Chat... and failed again. The company keeps trying, failing and succeeding with new products. Some stick – Chrome, Maps, Translate, Nest – and some don't. All in a decade's work!

In terms of an individual's career, it helps to see it as a series of taking a shot, and sometimes scoring a goal, and sometimes not. What matters is the kicking itself and having a sense of humour about those shots that missed the mark. I have heard some of the most famous designers in the world say, 'Oh my God, my Spring/Summer 2012 collection was awful! What was I thinking?' If I, as a publicist, wept over the beauty of every single collection, the designers would call BS on me. It can't *all* be 'Breathtaking, darling...'

Honest opinion can be given with empathy (feeling how they feel) and compassion (caring how they feel). Being too blunt could read as heartless, which would be devastating as well as offensive. My white elephant strategy is to have a difficult discussion over a glass of wine or a cup of coffee when possible, in private, to give them my full attention, and speak from a place of genuine care about what I truly believe is best for them and their brand. When I've been on the receiving end, I appreciate it when an unhappy client takes a moment to talk to me and explain their dissatisfaction in a thoughtful way, appreciating that they know I wouldn't have done anything to upset them on purpose but that, sometimes, things go wrong. I can then choose to defend our position or apologize and work out what to do next, in a mutually respectful way.

Often, though, there is no option and these frank conversations take place in a crowded conference room. I've walked out of meetings, my legs shaking, thinking, *Did I really just say that out loud to a client in a room full of people?* Very often, my team has the same reaction, coming up to me afterwards with shocked expressions, saying, 'I can't believe you just said that!'

During a meeting with a magazine editor about a new fragrance we were launching for a client, I said, 'It's a very musky, powerful fragrance. Personally, I don't like it, but I think there's a big market for it.' The editor just burst out laughing and said, 'You've got to be the only PR person out there who comes in and says the truth, which is that not everybody likes every fragrance. Nothing more subjective than fragrance! Normally, they say, "It's so incredible, so amazing." And I'm like, "Who are you kidding? Get real."'

The honesty paid off. She wrote beautifully about the fragrance, but at the same time acknowledged that it was not for everyone. It's a beauty industry basic that different nationalities and parts of the world love very difference fragrances. The client was thrilled. You don't lose anything by being honest when it comes from a place of care.

Appearances Speak Volumes

It seems obvious, and yet I've had strained conversations with staff members about how their grooming and style communicates the wrong message to colleagues and clients. We might be wading into politically incorrect territory, and I'm sorry for that, but the truth is, to some extent, we are all in the image business. The last thing we want to do is to project a disregard for appearances. Whether it's a CEO, a software engineer or a dog walker, how one chooses to look sends a message. At TCS, employees are asked to be well-groomed and to dress neatly. No grubby clothes, dirty nails or body odour.

Even as a fashion and beauty PR company, I don't expect our staff to be done up to the nines. Being stylish is difficult and rare, and, in my view, it takes a lot of effort, time and thought. I'm not great at it and our teams don't have to be either, but they do have to make a modicum of effort. People will be making snap judgements about how you look. If you don't acknowledge and appreciate that fact, you limit your job opportunities and potential.

Looking workplace-appropriate demonstrates consideration and respect to the clients. If staffers show up for a meeting with a five-star hotel group in tattered tracksuit bottoms and ripped shirts, we might send them home to change. If the head of a bank is coming in, I have to tell them, 'Sorry, guys, we've got to insist on a jacket right now.' An hour later, when an exec of a Millennial make-up brand arrives, the jackets come off. (I've been called 'schoolmarmish' for my sartorial criticisms.) I've even sent people into the showers for a shampoo before a meeting with a haircare client whose brand was all about healthy, clean, gorgeous hair!

The way one stands, sits and holds oneself might send disrespectful and inconsiderate signals as well. One man in my office had the habit of sitting down at the table and opening his legs – wide. The people seated on either side had to move their chairs to avoid his knees. But that was only the physical problem, not the more important symbolic one. Was he oblivious, selfish or trying to tell us all what a big man he was with this posture? None of those prospects were flattering: his seated position made females feel particularly uncomfortable. I would have been embarrassed to ask him about it in front of everyone, so after a meeting I went over to him and simply said, 'Listen, forgive me, but I need to tell you something. Please don't be offended. It's just that the way you sit in meetings makes me feel uncomfortable and I know that it is crowding other people at the table, too.'

I didn't make a big deal of it and he seemed genuinely surprised to hear that he was taking up more space than he ought to and apologized immediately. I doubt anyone in his life had ever corrected this man about his posture. The conversation was awkward, but necessary. After we had our little chat, he changed his ways for good. And now his body language is respectful and allows people to pay attention to what he is saying, not how he's sitting.

Apart from attire, grooming and posture, there's self-care. Some people in the office frankly party hard (as one does in one's twenties). Sometimes, they come in tired and hungover, and the rest, which can communicate skewed priorities. Being so incapacitated by the previous night's fun that you can't do your job does not inspire confidence in your co-workers or your boss. If you look (or smell) like you've come straight to the office from the pub or club, please just keep on walking.

We had an all-company meeting recently, and one of the guys fell asleep in his chair. I pulled him aside and I said, 'Listen, don't come to the office to sleep because you've been partying too hard. It's not appropriate. You are an ambassador for this company at all times.' Duly shamed, he didn't do it again.

It's very awkward to have these types of conversations, but I'm used to it by now. Communication is a two-way street. When I send someone home to sleep it off or change their clothes, I'm letting them know, with compassion and honesty, that they are sending the wrong message to our clients. I also try to communicate the right way to conduct oneself. Part of my homework is to dress well and appear alert all the time during the workday. When I'm at home, I put on my ripped old-lady T-shirts, tracksuit bottoms and slippers. My favourite shoes of all are my FitFlops. Marcia Kilgore, the brand's founder, is an entrepreneur and marketer I hugely admire. I love it that she makes some of the most comfortable shoes in the world, and the world is now getting to a better place – back in the old days offices were more about high heels, now

FitFlops and other super comfortable shoes are totally work-appropriate, thank goodness.

Don't Underestimate the Written Word

In 2017, journalist Lucy Kellaway wrote an article about, as she described it, 'corporate claptrap' and provided a series of obtuse business's statements, slogans and press releases.[5] Here are some good examples:

> From the founder of a major coffee chain about a new product that would be, 'Delivering an immersive, ultra-premium, coffee-forward experience.'
>
> From the CEO of a large ad agency: 'As brands build out a world footprint, they look for the no-holds-barred global POV that's always been part of our wheelhouse.'
>
> From the CEO of a large apparel company: 'In the wholesale channel, [our brand] exited doors not aligned with brand status and invested in presentations through both enhanced, assortments and dedicated, customized real estate in key doors.'

I'm still trying to figure out what any of them were talking about!

Kellaway noted how some companies take a simple concept and make it needlessly confusing, such as Toyota rebranding a car as a 'sustainable mobility solution', Amazon calling a book a 'reading container' and Nestlé's bottled water an 'affordable portable lifestyle beverage'. It all reads and sounds like total BS, doesn't it?

At TCS, the press releases I like the best have no 'bests' in them, are less than one page long and are factual. They're not Shakespeare, but they should just provide useful, truthful information.

As for emails, a common mistake people make is being too casual and personal. So many executive level people have told me how put off they are when they open an email from a complete stranger that starts, 'Hi, Jane!' or 'Heya, Eric! How's your summer been?' instead of 'Dear Ms or Mr So-and-So' or 'I hope this email finds you well.' An initial email should be just as formal as a first face-to-face introduction. The writing should follow the same rules for spoken language: be clear, brief and grateful. I usually include a 'thank you' at the top and the bottom of every email. Most people are busy, and time is money. Good manners, grammar and spelling are as important today as ever before. Errors are a huge red flag that you didn't pay attention to detail. If someone is slapdash in a professional text, email or tweet, she might cut corners in other ways as well.

In our omnichannel, multiplatform changing world, going back to basics stands out. No one remembers an email, but a handwritten letter will get their attention. It shows that you took time and care, and that kind of special attention is always appreciated. I went to a dinner hosted by CEW (Cosmetic Executive Women) UK, of which I am an Executive Board member. Tracey Woodward, then the CEO of Aromatherapy Associates and fellow board member, was there. She provided goody bags for thirty people with beautiful products for us to take home. I'm sure many attendees sent her an email the next day. To make a deeper impression, I wrote a letter – paper and ink – to thank her, said it was always great to see her and that I'd used her products and was grateful for them. The next time I saw her, she seemed very happy to chat. Little things, like handwriting thank you notes, count.

Since texting has largely replaced calling, a polite call might stand out, too. In the early days, I made hundreds of cold calls a week. With dignity, respectfulness, humility and proper manners, I'd say, 'Good morning. This is Julietta from The Communications Store. How are you? Is this a good moment to speak, or am I disturbing you...'

Invariably, the editors would brush me off, saying, 'Sorry, I'm on a deadline' or 'I can't talk. I have to take my cat to the vet.'

I kept a detailed log of every call and every editor's reason for not talking to me. The following week, I'd call back and say, 'I'm sorry to trouble you again and I hope you met your deadline last week' or 'How's your cat?'

They'd say, 'How did you remember that?' and it was my way in. I'd get two minutes of their time to pitch the product and would make the most of it. Cold calls don't have to be chilly; with warmth and thoughtfulness – and active listening – it's possible to connect on a human level and communicate that there is a real person with a beating heart on the other end, not a robo-calling machine.

I'm not going to give a long lecture about proper mobile phone etiquette. At TCS, our policy is not to use them in meetings unless you need your phone to show the client something.

I remember having one meeting with clothing retailer Boden CEO Johnnie Boden and another one of his advisors. The advisor kept his phone on the table. A notification popped up about an important political news item. I can't remember what the news was, maybe a politician's shocking resignation, and he interrupted our discussion to say, 'Oh my God. Look at that! Did you know?'

Johnnie said (somewhat jokingly), 'Really! If I was paying you to read headlines or keep me up to speed on political news, I would have let you know. Please put your phone away. I need your attention and advice – that is what I am paying you for.'

If I am being paid by a client for my time, I try hard to give them my undivided attention. Full stop. No matter what else I communicate to whomever I do business with, it's about appreciation and respect.

Communications is a huge aspect of business and encompasses every way people interact with each other, from how they sit, stand, talk, listen and look, to sending 'vibes' about thoughts and intentions, writing, calling, behaviour, delivering good and bad news, and managing expectations. So much goes into every conversation and email exchange, with so much room for interpretation on both ends. As long as everyone understands that, like it or not, every word and punctuation mark makes an impression, they can slow down and take extra care to send the message they want others to receive: 'I care about you. I care about myself. I am here to get the job done.'

COMMUNICATIONS

What you say, do, write and wear speaks volumes about you to the people you work with. If you are to get across a single, clear message – that you are a no-BS person – stick with these strategies:

- If your boss asks you to lie or cheat in an act of 'truthful hyperbole', RESIST! Honesty in communication is the only policy.
- Make 'realness' your super power. People can smell 'fake' in a heartbeat. To communicate authenticity, be the same person wherever you are, whoever you're with.
- Language is the first line of communication. Don't blag it. Speak with precision, cite specific details and don't waste words.
- Clever is good; clear is better in meetings. If a client or the boss fails to appreciate your humour, the joke's on you.
- Keep it clean! No swearing, even if the client, colleague or boss goes there first.
- When asking questions, use 'what' instead of 'why' to avoid a confrontational tone.
- Deliver bad news as quickly as possible. It's always worse if they hear it from someone else first.
- Have the guts to call out the white elephant in the room, but do it with kindness and care.
- Wash your hair, clean your nails and dress in a way that's not offensive to humans.

- All written correspondence should be as precise and clear as spoken language. Take care with grammar, spelling and tone.
- Always communicate gratitude in every conversation or correspondence.
- Whether you're doing it face-to-face or by email or message, consider how your words will be interpreted by others.
- Strive for grateful, respectful and open.

4 Service

When one thinks about BS customer service, air travel often hits the top of the charts. Whether it's charging for extra checked baggage or making people sit in a plane for hours on the tarmac without food or water, or losing animals in cargo holds, airlines sometimes seem to get more wrong than right in how they treat passengers.

Poor customer service hit a new low when Flybmi, a British regional airline, went into administration in February 2019, abruptly cancelling all of its flights and leaving hundreds of passengers stranded. The lucky passengers who were able to reroute on different airlines wound up travelling and transferring for many hours for what should have been a quick hop. What offended so many was that the airline didn't give the passengers any warning. Some people posted on social media that they learned about the cancelled flights from their news feeds, not directly from the airline itself. And even while there was chaos at regional airports as people tried to figure out alternative plans, the airline's website continued to book flights and advertise deals.[1] Adding insult to injury, those passengers are unlikely to be compensated for their troubles or reimbursed for the fares of the cancelled flights. Flybmi owed £37 million at the time of its collapse. According to administrators, the airline's creditors might get back only 1 per cent of what they are owed.[2] In a statement, Flybmi blamed Brexit uncertainty and rising fuel costs for its troubles, but offered no words of apology to its rightfully angry passengers. Even if it hadn't run out of cash, I wonder if Flybmi would have lasted anyway. No company can survive by putting its customers last.

In 2016, TCS opened a New York office. Some US staffers were at that time a little fascinated by *Downton Abbey* and the Royal Family. I think they were interested in the tradition of generational servitude in England. I told them that *Downton Abbey* was a period piece about changing times, and that the way of life depicted in the show was a thing of the past. However, the concept of being 'in service' is as relevant today as it was 100 years ago. We all hope to find a job that serves some purpose, at the very least. Ideally, the purpose would be noble and improve people's lives. Being 'in service' doesn't mean servitude. It's about being useful and feeling passionate about the service one provides – along with getting paid.

As a business leader, I subscribe to the 'servant leader' ideology of serving my staff. As a publicist, my job is to serve my clients and their purpose by promoting their products and endeavours, which, in turn, serves their customers. To that end, our objective at TCS is to give our clients a bit more than what they expect to make things just that little bit better than our competitors. I chose this industry, in part, because it's in my nature to want to please people. I'll admit it – when I know I've done right by my clients, I feel a sense of accomplishment which is its own reward.

For some senior people, ego gets in the way. They might believe they are too good or important to be of service to others, and that helping, caring and sharing is somehow beneath them. They see service as demeaning themselves for the benefit of others. (In reality, it is the opposite.) This profoundly damaging attitude can be found at every level of business. A hierarchical office structure promotes it. Senior people expect their colleagues – and sometimes clients – to serve them.

GET OVER YOURSELF

No matter what your role in the company, or what level you are, you are serving someone, be it the most 'senior' or 'junior' person, the client, the customer or the shareholders. You have someone to please and answer to, and that person will be happier with you if you are doing what you can to serve them well. This has nothing to do with lowering yourself for someone else. It's about taking pride in your role and understanding how you contribute to the greater whole. If you're going to do a job, you should do it to the very best of your ability.

I often think about waiting tables, the ultimate service job. In Italy, being a waiter is considered a prestigious profession. Italians love food! Imagine going to a restaurant where the waiter explains the menu with passion, is proud of the food he is serving and loves his job. Then imagine going to a restaurant where the waiter never makes eye contact, can barely describe the food and gives off the impression that he's counting the minutes until he can clock off. You'll have a totally different experience, even if the same food comes out of the kitchen.

The health and growth of your career as an individual, and your company as a whole, depends on the quality of the service you provide to colleagues, bosses and clients. If you fulfil your purpose to make other people happy, and do your very best for them, you'll feel profound gratification. And your business will flourish, too.

If You Don't Care About Them, They Won't Care About You

According to one report, poor customer service cost UK companies £37 billion in 2017.[3] That year, customers logged 55 million gripes. In four out of five cases, if those complaints were not handled properly, customers vowed to take their business elsewhere. Twenty-eight per cent of consumers will abandon their brand loyalty after one bad experience with customer service and, among the younger generation, brand loyalty is even more precarious. Sixty-three per cent of consumers are resigned to how badly they'll be treated, and have lost faith that companies will do what's right for them despite the endless, empty promises advertised. And loyalty, by its very definition, is a long-term activity. If a boyfriend or girlfriend is true for only one week, it doesn't mean much!

In an era of infinite choice, maintaining brand loyalty is essential – and it might very well come down to how much a company cares about customer experience. People need to feel that their issues have been heard and taken seriously, whether it's in a marriage, a friendship, a professional relationship or a relationship with a brand. If they sense that their opinions matter, they'll stick with the relationship. If a boss or a colleague shows they care about their client, co-workers or customers, it's human nature to reciprocate in kind.

Know What You're Selling and Whom You're Serving

The online shoe and clothing retailer Zappos is an excellent example of a company that puts customer service at the top of its priorities. CEO Tony Hsieh once wrote, 'Zappos is a customer service company that just happens to sell shoes.'[4] Zappos has some legendary customer service stories, like the time a phone rep sent flowers to a customer who wanted to return shoes she had bought for her recently deceased mother, or when a rep spoke to a customer for ten-and-a-half hours straight (it would have been rude to cut her off). Obviously, during that long call, the rep wasn't handling any other business and, in that sense, it might not have been an efficient use of time. However, the tale of that call made headlines and has been driving traffic and customers to the site for years.

Zappos can't compete with online giants or bricks-and-mortar chain discounters on price points. So, they don't try. Instead, the company promises to 'wow' customers whenever they interact with the company via email, phone or chat. They encourage customer interaction and display the 1-800 number on every page of the site, inviting friendly interactions.

Emily Weiss, CEO and founder of the cosmetics company Glossier, was so attuned to her customers' needs that she crowdsourced opinions and engaged directly with customers online to create products that addressed their needs and wants, for example a non-sticky sunscreen lotion. In an interview with *Entrepreneur* magazine, she said, 'So many people on Instagram [wrote] to say, "Thank you so much for listening; we've been waiting for this moment."'[5] Glossier's customer service department is devoted to collecting feedback from customers, replying to their comments and questions with passion and originality.

At TCS, we aren't selling shoes or make-up; we are selling service and experience. My business partner Daniel always challenges me to 'surprise and delight' our clients with an attention to detail and willingness to do anything for them. He believes this is what customers really want. He goes the endless extra mile for our clients. He has been known to walk clients' shoes round to the concierge of a nearby hotel to make sure they look perfect, right before an event that the client has put their every last ounce of energy in to. Daniel is the master of any VIP event – he himself manages the front row of some of the greatest fashion shows on the planet with his team. His humble love and passion to serve those around him knows no bounds. Finding what in French is called '*le plaisir de server*' is core, and demonstrates real passion and care.

Trust Every Member of the Team to Serve Well

Serving means caring, which is one of TCS's core values. All too often in the world, you see evidence of not caring in the glassy eyes of salespeople, in phone service agents who hang up on customers, in airlines that bump people off flights, in PR execs overpromising and under-delivering to their clients, in bosses who don't care about the emotional needs of their staff. Apathy has a trickle-down effect. Poor customer service is very often the result of apathetic leadership. People emulate the behaviours they see in management. If a shop salesperson barely acknowledges the customers, and says a rote, 'Hi, how are you today?', I guarantee you that person is reacting to how she has been treated by her supervisor. On the other hand, if a salesperson rushes to help customers with their wet umbrellas and goes out of her way to look after them, she is most likely demonstrating the caring and kindness she has received. To the customer, it's a vital difference. And the customer is whom everyone in business is there to serve.

When a company respects and trusts people at every level, it gives them the power to serve well. The Ritz-Carlton Hotel Company has a policy that every employee – from the receptionist, to housekeeping, to food service workers – has the authority to spend $2000 per day per guest to make the customer experience of a random guest exceptional. It might mean sending a bottle of champagne to someone's table or upgrading their room. It's about the customer, of course, but also engaging employees to be their very best. Ritz-Carton COO and president Herve Humler told *Forbes*, 'I believe in the power of recognition and empowerment leading to great employee engagement. And employee engagement is critical to guest engagement.'[6] Good idea.

American author and economist Paul J. Zak, director of the Center for Neuroeconomic Studies, has been studying the intersection of trust and neurophysiology in the business world for two decades and wrote in his book *Trust Factor*, 'Colleagues who reported higher levels of trust had statistically significant more Joy, were more likely to agree with the organization's Purpose, had more energy at work and said they were more productive. Trust also increased closeness to colleagues and substantially reduced chronic stress.' According to his stats, the 25 per cent of employees who reported the highest level of trust in the organization were 21 per cent more productive than those at the bottom 25 per cent. People at high-trust companies overall were found to have more energy, satisfaction and engagement at work, and less stress, fewer sick days and less burnout.[7]

When the CEO makes it the company's official policy to let their employees follow their own best judgement, is it any wonder that they feel well served by that leadership and will pass along the good vibes to the customer? It's basic human nature that if you give people the freedom to do well, the vast majority of them will strive to be worthy of that trust and respect.

ONE MORE TIME, WITH FEELING

Being of service means providing something of value for someone else. You put them before you. If that value is emotionally based – you supply a feeling of happiness, security and comfort – the more impactful and memorable your service will be. You transfer positive energy from yourself to another. You give. As you advance along your career path, you will serve yourself well by remembering that your number one job is to make the people you work with – inside and outside the company – feel good. What people crave in their heart of hearts is acknowledgment and appreciation. By keeping those words in mind, you can build strong professional networks, and even a billion-pound company.

Be Patient

There have been many times in my career when my service instinct, and patience, has been tested. Clients show up at our office to discuss how to take their brand to the next level. We are tasked with coming up with five to ten strategies to help them achieve their goals. We work very hard and present our ideas to the client, hoping they'll choose a strategy or two, so we can begin to implement it. But they are often unable to make a decision.

It's impossible to talk about making people feel acknowledged and appreciated without patience. Patience is a kindness, and it's also a practice, something that you have to learn over and over again. Impatience, on the other hand, puts people on edge. The objective is to make colleagues and clients feel happy and secure. Rushing them along will only make them nervous, and they'll come to associate a co-worker's disservice of impatience with that uncomfortable feeling.

When waiting to hear from a client or a boss about something important, the impatient strategy would be to say, 'When do you think you'll make a decision?' The patient strategy would be to ask, 'Is there anything you need or want from me? How can I make this easier for you? Thank you so much.' It's the difference between a push and a nudge. I've found that people respond better to the gentler approach.

Sometimes we can get super frustrated with clients. We've literally given them multiple ideas that never quite land, and then we don't get the contract. Team members vent to me and say, 'That client is *so* annoying, they're just pumping us for ideas but they're never really going to hire us.' Sometimes that is true, but my view is different. Actually, we have not managed to persuade the client 100 per cent that our idea is brilliant or presented it in a way that makes them want to sign that contract and let us execute it for them. If we didn't get the deal, we failed to serve them what they needed from us. Even if their behaviour wasn't perfect, it's still on us. Of course, there are also those cases where the client is simply not ready to hear or accept an idea for one reason or another, and that's nothing to do with the pitch at all.

RESIST THE URGE TO DAZZLE

The real test of anyone in a service industry – which we are nearly all in – is being able to suppress the urge to be the star. We need to read a situation, pick up on the energy and respond accordingly. You might need to take the lead, or just sit quietly and listen. If you sense that the client is waiting to be impressed, then go ahead and plunge in. But, more often than not, the client does not want to sit there and listen to you. They want a back-and-forth, substantive and collaborative conversation.

Serve clients by reading the room, listening to what they say (and don't say) and taking steps to fulfil their needs. Video conferencing makes this *very* hard. And I have been in many meetings where the technology simply doesn't allow humans to read each other. When possible, try to meet face-to-face. Otherwise, just do your best to clue in.

If you bring emotional awareness into your professional relationships, you will be sought out for your insight and be appreciated for having it. But if you push yourself forward and don't tune into the client's needs, you'll be regarded as someone who can't help, and no one wants to work with that person. There are a number of kinds of intelligence but, in any field, the one you need most is emotional intelligence.

Be Passionate

I remember once walking a group of reporters through a five-star hotel that had just opened – the exquisite Hotel de Russie in Rome. Sir Rocco Forte, our client and the owner and founder of Rocco Forte Hotels, was waiting patiently to take our journalist guests to dinner. He looked up and noticed that a bulb had blown in the reception area's chandelier. He quickly asked for a ladder, climbed up it and changed the bulb as our guests came down from their rooms. You bet that made an impression on the journalists! Talk about service.

Once, at a big press event for John Frieda haircare in Turks and Caicos, John thought it would be so beautiful if each of the sunloungers around the private pool was laced in bougainvillea (a gorgeous flowering plant). I got up at 4 a.m. to set to work so that we'd be ready for the 9 a.m. press launch. Only one person was there at that time, John himself, helping me to decorate each lounger. He demonstrates passion for his work with his attention to detail and willingness to do any task, no matter how menial. This manifestation of passion is a vital and common thread I've seen in the most successful people out there. They are never too busy or too important to do the work.

It's the same with the visionary founder of NET-A-PORTER, Dame Natalie Massenet. I remember sitting on the floor in Natalie's first office when she started the online luxury clothing retailer. She was standing in front of an ironing board, smoothing the now-iconic black tissue paper that goes inside the boxes. I wasn't surprised when NET-A-PORTER became the world's most successful online fashion business.

Why would all of these iconic leaders do the grunt work when they could easily hire or enlist someone else to do it for them? The answer is that truly wise businesspeople understand that no matter how theoretically high up they get, they are always in the service of their customers. Another humble and passionate leader I've had the privilege of working with is Johnnie Boden of the online clothing store Boden. He's never given himself a day to think about how successful he's been, but instead he focuses on how his brand can evolve, be better and be more useful to his customers. And yes, I've been in a room when he fixated on what colour ribbon detail to put on a skirt. Paul Smith, who's made millions from his eponymous clothing business, takes a little piece of cardboard and winds different coloured wool threads around it to create his world-famous striped products. He could easily give that to a team of designers or rely on CGI to do it for him, but he passionately, creatively does it himself.

At our office, there is no such thing as a menial job. I have packed many press or gift bags shoulder-to-shoulder with the younger staff. If any job is good enough for them, it's good enough for me. I hope that, one day, when they become the CEO of their own company, they'll also write place cards and thank you notes side-by-side with their staff. If you have not done the job yourself, how can you ask someone else to do it and know what is required?

A shoddily written report or a dashed off email shows a lack of regard for the recipient. I have a litmus test for quality that we call 'the Chanel test'. Chanel is one of the last privately owned luxury goods companies in the world, known for its impeccable beauty and attention to detail in everything that bears its name. You won't see a Chanel goody bag, a thank you note, a presentation put together with anything but the ultimate care. Whenever I see bags of products going out of our doors, I ask myself if they would pass the Chanel test, and, if not, they should be redone.

A passionate worker at any level gets down and picks up a piece of rubbish in their shop. Less evolved, less passionate people would say, 'Get someone to clean that up!' They've lost their hunger, curiosity and humility. If I ever started to think that other people were there to serve me rather than me being there to serve them, I pray someone will give me the heads-up and push me to quit and start all over again.

I'm very clear in my own mind that the energy one brings into a room has a contagious effect. Energy transference is real; there is no doubt that we all project something, be it negative or positive, and that our energy has an enormous impact on those around us. I take care to enter a room and bring with me what those in that room might find useful, happy and positive. If I dragged myself in there, gloomy and down, everyone would immediately absorb that energy, worry that something was wrong and then react defensively. When I come in with my head up and my shoulders square and say, 'Good morning! How is everyone today?' they feel reassured that we're going to have a productive meeting. By being present and bright, anyone can reinforce teamwork and put others in a good mood. However, it's important to say here that this is easier said than done – it's no walk in the park to do this day in, day out. Everyone is human and everyone has bad days – it's hard not to drag difficult issues from home or family life into the office. There have been days when I've had to dig so deep to be there for everyone; I don't want to pretend that it's easy.

It's possible to change the dynamic in someone's attitude with just a few, well-meaning words. In his book *Jack Welch and the GE Way*, author Robert Slater described an experiment they tried at General Electric (GE) to test how friendliness can impact efficiency. One group of GE phone operators answered customer calls with a cheerful greeting, like, 'Hello! Good morning! How can I help you today?' The other operators were more succinct and a bit chilly, saying just, 'General Electric'. The operators who opened with an upbeat, albeit longer, greeting completed the calls in less time. The company made more money due to the efficiency, and the customers reported greater satisfaction.

Just a few sincere sentences can change someone's disposition. It's all in the intonation of voice. Apathy breeds frustration and isolation; positivity multiplies and spreads. Life is too short to surround ourselves with people who drag us all down with negative energy.

BE QUICK ABOUT IT

On a purely practical level, good service means two things: speed and efficiency. If a company's service is slow and undependable, don't be surprised if it's taken to task on Yelp or Twitter.

When I was first starting out, I had a thirty-minute rule. If I was, say, pitching one of our clients' new products to a magazine and the editor called with a question about the product, I promised to call back with an answer within thirty minutes, and did, every time. Even if I didn't have all the information the editor needed, I called back after half an hour with an update. I'd explain that I was doing all I could to collect the full information, had some of it already and would be back with the rest.

Nothing is quite so frustrating as being left hanging. Again, it goes back to making people feel acknowledged and appreciated – the opposite of neglected. By being on time and delivering on promises ASAP, you will make the client or customer feel important. Even better, they will know that they can rely on you. Bottom line: you care. When you treat others well and can be counted on, you are building trust, which is an invaluable asset.

Serve Like Your Livelihood Depends on It (Which It Does)

Whenever money changes hands, there's an element of distrust. Will this person do what I'm paying them to do? Will this investment pay off? If that fear is removed from the transaction by being an excellent service provider, clients will be happy to part with their well-earned money.

When TCS tried to win the John Frieda haircare account back in 1999, I was on maternity leave. Tom had a good meeting with John and his incredible business partner Gail Federici, but they wouldn't give us their business without meeting me, too.

Soon after, I met John at a top London hotel, carrying a briefcase to try to look important. I also wore a pinstripe suit! John asked me what I realistically thought I could do for the brand. I took out a blank piece of paper and wrote on it what I thought we could do. In fear of overpromising and under-delivering, I knew we could accomplish 100 per cent of what I wrote, but I thought I could probably do 30 per cent more. John took the paper, folded it and put it in his breast pocket. He said, 'We'll pay you £5000 a month for twelve months if you do all of these things. If you achieve it all by this time next year, we'll double your fees. No need for a lengthy contract. I've got this piece of paper.' He patted his pocket. Five thousand a month was amazing money for us. This was a pivotal win for a tiny start-up; if we hadn't had this commitment, we might not have made it. We are genuinely indebted to John and Gail.

Tom and I, and our small team, worked like dogs and delivered on every item on the list, plus the 30 per cent I didn't include. A year to the day later, I was working side-by-side with John to prepare for a press event, checking on minute details (as I said, he always goes the extra mile to make things perfect). I didn't even remember that it'd been a year since our first meeting because we were so busy with the event.

He said, 'By the way, Julietta, as promised, TCS's fees have been changed.' He didn't stop what he was doing or even look up. It was a seamless, elegant, beautiful, unforgettable moment – and the beginning of a twenty-year working relationship between us. I was realistic and reliable, and John worked harder than any of us and set the example.

If we hadn't gone the extra mile for John and secured his ongoing commitment to us, who knows what might have happened. We needed the business, and we did what we needed to do, and then some, to keep it. When looking back at pivotal moments in a decades-long career, it seems obvious that when someone gives as much as they can, they (usually) get what they deserve. Though, that said...

Take Pride in Good Work, Even If It's Not Acknowledged

Even if you provide excellent service, a stubborn few clients, bosses or customers will never be happy. Anyone who has ever worked in retail or the food industry is well aware of this fact. It's true in corporate business, too. The top-shelf quality service one provides to clients, bosses and co-workers will be appreciated and applauded nine times out of ten, but I always say, 'there's always one' who will never be satisfied.

There have been times in our company history when we've cut ties with clients because we know they are dissatisfied. Most often, it's due to a lack of understanding of how our service works and because of unrealistic expectations. Clients come with a preconceived idea of what success looks like without sharing it or being open about it. Sometimes, they appoint a PR and communications team because they just want to be famous. There's nothing wrong with that, but we prefer to build brands than indulge egos and are super proud to represent the people behind the brands and the product they are trying to sell.

At the end of the day, the key to excellent service is about pride in oneself and one's work. All the other factors I've talked about – the passion, enthusiasm, patience, humility and reliability – will flow freely if their source comes from genuine pride in whom or what you're serving. Even more than finding one's bliss, if people can find a calling that gives them that sense of pride, they will go forth and do wonders. Work won't feel like work.

SERVICE

Want to provide the best quality service to everyone you do business with, from your boss, to your clients, customers and colleagues, but don't know where to start? The following tips will give you a solid foundation to work from:

- Put whomever you're serving – the client, customer or boss – first.
- Acknowledge and appreciate others to make meaningful, memorable connections.
- Give everyone the freedom and respect to serve in their way, and they will rise to the highest of expectations.
- Listen to what others are saying, and use insight and instinct to hear what they might not have the words to say.
- Serve your clients' interests, not yours.
- Patience sets you apart. Emotional control is a rare value these days, and you'll stand out if you can keep your cool.

- Do everything with the utmost care, even so-called 'menial' tasks.
- Energy is contagious. Positivity will improve people's attitudes.
- Speed and efficiency shouldn't be at the expense of quality.

5 Money

When I tried to come up with the most egregious example of unethical corporate greed, one man instantly came to mind.

In 2015, Martin Shkreli, a thirty-one-year-old entrepreneur, started up the company Turing Pharmaceuticals and promptly purchased the rights to the drug Daraprim. Daraprim had been around for decades as a treatment for toxoplasmosis, a parasitic infection that can be dangerous for pregnant women and fatal for patients with compromised immune systems due to AIDs or chemotherapy. The price of the drug before Shkreli acquired it was $13.50 per pill. Overnight, he raised the price to $750 per pill, a fifty-fold increase.

In reaction to this price increase, there were widespread protests by medical associations. Shkreli was excoriated in the media and portrayed as a greedy, uncaring 'Pharma Bro' who set out to profit from the most weak and vulnerable members of society. Shkreli's defence was that Turing needed to turn a profit to develop new versions of the drug, but that was met with scorn, since the old version worked well.[1] After the public outcry, the price was dropped to $375 per pill, still significantly higher and out of reach for most patients.

Three months later, Shkreli resigned from Turing after he was arrested in New York on charges of fraud unrelated to the drug-pricing scandal. From 2009 to 2014, he ran hedge fund MSMB Capital Management and convinced investors to pour cash into another pharmaceutical company – Retrophin – which Shkreli used as his personal piggy bank. The company was a shell, and investors were cheated out of $11 million. In 2018, Shkreli's crimes caught up with him. He was convicted of two counts of securities fraud and sentenced to seven years in prison. He called the trial 'a silly witch-hunt perpetrated by self-serving prosecutors'.[2] I suppose he does know a bit about being 'self-serving'.

Profit over people – one hears that phrase a lot in business. As far as money is concerned – and it is, of course, a great concern to everyone in business, as it should be – my central philosophy is 'people *and* profit'. It is more important to us at TCS to be fair and honest in all our financial dealings than it is to just rake it in above anything else.

I was once discussing whether to hire a chief financial officer with Craig Cohon, traveller, business owner, the man who brought Coca-Cola and Cirque du Soleil to Russia, and chairman of Worn Again Technologies, a brilliant B2B business that is working so cleverly to recycle mixed textiles that otherwise go into landfill; a real game changer. He said to me, 'You don't need a CFO, you need a CWO – a chief wealth officer – because wealth is not just about money.'

I have come to understand that integrity, compassion and an ethical reputation are the true wealth of anyone in business.

Such capital doesn't come and go like money. I would rather make less if financial gains required us to be dishonourable to our clients, our people or as a representative in our industry.

Short-term Greed Does Not Pay Off

Any unscrupulous financial practice, any one profit-over-people decision, can critically damage or destroy a global brand, or an industry as a whole.

Thanks to the Great Recession, people have learned to be cynical about corporate responsibility, as they should be. Shady, greedy deals and financial products caused the 2008 financial crisis and almost destroyed the global economy. We're not going to get into the ethics of subprime mortgages here, but suffice it to say, banks knowingly lending money that would eventually lock customers into a kind of financial servitude is not ethical or sustainable. Many banks in the US and the UK closed (Lehman Brothers) or were acquired by the government or larger banks (Bear Stearns, Merrill Lynch, HBOS, Royal Bank of Scotland, Bradford & Bingley and Fortis). The bank failures were a good example of how short-term greed can do long-term damage.

You could look a bit further back to find the root cause of the recession in corrupt record-keeping at companies that thought they could get away with anything – 'cooking the books' and deceiving shareholders. By the way, many of these executives were promoted, incentivized and celebrated for doing exactly that. The Texas energy company Enron was huge, with 22,000 employees, hundreds of thousands of shareholders and revenues of $101 billion (or so they claimed). In 2000, *Fortune* named it one of the '100 Best Companies to Work for in America'. A year later, *Forbes* named it 'America's Most Innovative Company'.[3] As it turned out, Enron's greatest innovation was fraud. With premier US accounting firm Arthur Andersen's help, Enron grossly inflated and/or completely made up assets and profits. Before the real numbers were uncovered, Enron executives with insider knowledge started selling stock in massive amounts, taking their profit before it all blew up. In 2001, the truth came out and both Enron and Arthur Andersen collapsed. Entire towns full of people were suddenly unemployed, with Enron stock worthless. Shareholders lost all of their investment. Many of the execs who led the company to ruin were fined millions; some were convicted of financial crimes and sent to prison.[4] But this was cold comfort to all the people who were deceived into believing in the company and wound up losing their jobs and their retirement savings.

Even in the post-recession banking world, some companies are doing some unscrupulous accounting. In 2015, Wells Fargo employees, under pressure to meet sales goals, created millions of fake accounts under real customers' names and upsold unnecessary financial products to unwitting customers. For their transgressions, in 2018, the bank reached a settlement with the US attorney general to pay $575 million on top of a previous fine of $1.2 billion.[5]

If not making up accounts outright, there are many ways to fraudulently inflate revenue and decrease debt to make a company appear to be more profitable than it is in order to meet quotas or drive up the share price. For example, a company could take in a one-time payment for multiple years of service but declare the entire amount as income for only the first year, thus inflating revenue. To decrease apparent debt, a company could hide some of it by moving it into a newly created subsidiary. There is really no end to what an unscrupulous and clever accountant can do.

Transparency Is Easier, Even When It's Hard

I've heard tales of some companies that juggle four sets of books – one for the government, one with the true figures, one for shareholders and one for lenders. Just maintaining two sets would be exhausting and confusing. Why not just be honest, and save everyone the time, energy and anxiety? Even during bad years, when the books aren't so pleasant, keep them open. Transparency is so much more streamlined – and steady – than deception.

At TCS, we have one set of accounts. The leadership team has full sight of its profit and loss numbers and works hard on them. Team leaders don't have a budget imposed on them. Instead, they build it and let us know if they are happy with what they hope to deliver for the coming year. On top of this, they share overall goals and ambitions with each other, so everyone knows what we are trying to achieve *together*. It is not without its complications because competition – sometimes healthy, sometimes not – does creep in.

I don't believe in saying business is booming every single year. It's just not true – that's not reality. Over the last twenty-four years, our profits have been anywhere from less than zero to 20 per cent. During the Great Recession, we had to take urgent and immediate action to safeguard our business. To get through a macroeconomic occurrence that we had no control over, I prioritized people over inanimate objects. So, we looked under the bonnet and tried to cut costs out of the business – anything from office supplies and flowers in reception to asking our people to take public transport rather than cabs. Anything to save jobs.

When we went back to work after Christmas in January 2009, the phone kept ringing with clients saying they just had to cut back and wanted to suspend our services, and so on. At that time in my career, I set my alarm at 5 a.m. to give myself two more hours of work every day to get through the crisis. What was I actually doing at 5 a.m.? Going back to basics. When a business grows, it is easy to forget the day-to-day basics – the crossing of t's and the dotting of i's. I was taking more time to review things to make sure they were correct, writing thank you notes to journalists for their continued support and sending reassuring emails to the staff saying how much we appreciated their hard work and dedication in a difficult time. As a side note, waking at 5 a.m. endless mornings in a row did start to take its toll. I got very tired and it certainly had an impact on my health. But it was an important contributing factor to getting the business through a tough time.

Thankfully, we had not stripped our profits out of the business every year and had left money in the bank 'for a rainy day'.

We were 'cash okay', so to speak. That allowed us to come up with a plan to quickly pre-empt the 'we're cutting back' phone calls. We called our key clients and made a proposal to reduce our fee to help them get through the crisis, retain their business and keep jobs at TCS. Once the governor of the Bank of England confirmed the country was out of recession, our clients would agree to get their fees back up to where they had been pre-recession, plus 5 per cent. What I learned was that the clients who left us altogether and did no PR and communications during that difficult economic period, pretty much disappeared. Those who continued, albeit at a reduced level, and traded through, came out the other side bigger, better, stronger, more beloved brands.

All of our clients honoured our agreement to reinstate fees after the recession, except one. And there's always one, right? When I raised the point of our fee adjustment, this particular client looked at me stunned, all perplexed, and said he had no recollection of that agreement at all. I brought the required paperwork to the table, signed by one of his senior staff members. That staff member had moved on (I wonder why) and therefore he immediately said that he could not honour a piece of paper signed by someone who had left his service. We 'resigned' this client and cut our losses.

As a CEO, you have to learn to bend with the wind or, rather, you have to learn how to be confident but not arrogant in the good years and have the ability to eat humble pie in the bad years. If we have a lean year and a potential client asks us about it, we can explain what happened and how we addressed the issue. Any wise person understands the cyclical nature of business. Every company has good years and not-so-great ones, so why not be honest about what we all know to be true? By being transparent, we gain trust with our clients and employees. Some clients find this honesty too difficult – they'd rather work with a company that says it's in 'great shape' all the time, whether it actually is or not. I understand that and respect that decision. However, what sometimes happens is that they learn the hard way that 'the grass is not always greener' or that it might be greener for a little while, but then a down cycle hits their new firm, too, just at a different time.

Charge a Fair Price for Honest Work

Establishing a reputation as a sustainable business that cares for its clients and its community is a 'return on ethics' that is more valuable than a return on investment. Ethics are an investment in long-term relationships. Clients trust companies that charge fairly and don't waste their money.

When the bank suits come and check on our finances, they always say we'd have better margins and greater profits if we were more ruthless. I know that, but I'd rather do it my way, on my no-BS terms. Despite this, regarding our billing practices, we are sometimes perceived as being quite expensive. Our fees are worth the face value of our services. As finance people have pointed out over the years, our 'over servicing' and doing more than we are contractually obliged to do take time away from lining up more business and making more money. To a degree, they're right... but I see that as short-termism, too. I'd still rather have the reputation of going above and beyond, than being thought of as doing only adequate work. Recommendations from happy clients are how we invest in our longevity.

In 2017, over 100 new business approaches strolled through our door, all through recommendations. We chose to pursue and pitch for half of them, and we were successful in landing 74 per cent of those. I thought this was an incredible achievement. We could have gone for more, we could charge more, but that would change the quality of our work and the trust we've built, as well as stress out the staff – and these people are already working very, very hard. Therefore, it wouldn't be sustainable. So, no go.

There are many people who charge huge fees and do as little as possible for the money. Very often, new clients say, 'We were with another agency and we paid them x amount and we didn't get anything for it. So why should be pay you y amount?' Good question. Anyone who sets fees should welcome the opportunity to justify what they charge, and then back it up with results. No-BS rates are based on a number of factors, including the company's (or individual freelancer's) track record, industry standards and the project budget, and should include a breakdown of how that figure was determined.

BS pricing is based on one major factor: what the BS company thinks it can get away with. That number might be higher or lower depending on the budget, but the calculations only take into account how to get the most while doing the least. From a client perspective, it's not too hard to figure out if the pricing is BS-based. A little pushback, such as, 'How did you come to this figure?' that sets off a stammered or unsubstantiated defence is the first clue.

An ethical company might actually do the most and get the least in certain situations. At the beginning of our business, when we had so much to prove to anyone who'd give us a chance, I said, 'We'll work for you for free for three months. If you like it, then we'll start billing you at x amount. If not, you can just walk away.' Today, that has evolved (we have to pay our salaries), but I find it hard to resist a small start-up that has little money but huge potential. In those cases, we structure fees that grow with the brand. I think it's reasonable to prove your worth before someone decides to mortgage their house to pay you. It only seems fair for both of us to operate on faith for a while. We've taken that bet over a dozen times over the years and have come out ahead 90 per cent of the time. Some people take the free work and never pay us a penny. That's their prerogative. If they stick with us, we build their brand, and ours, together. We form a relationship of trust and mutual appreciation, and, in the end, our loyal clients do our PR for us by telling others about our effort on their behalf.

Unheard of in BS businesses, I have been known to inform clients that they are overpaying and recommend reducing our fee. You should see the look on their faces! Sometimes, when we need to work in different ways, using different channels, or indeed a client has less going on for a while, we change our fees accordingly. With one client, I kept trying to schedule a meeting to discuss her fees, but she postponed it for months. I started to wonder why she would not see me and then I thought she probably assumed I was going to ask for *more* money and was trying to delay that discussion. When I told her that I wanted to reduce her fee, she started laughing because, if she'd taken the initial meeting, she would have been paying less for the last four months!

Treat Other People's Money Like Your Own

We tell our teams, 'Be creative and then work your budgets like no one's business.' If someone protests – 'I can't run a campaign with such a small budget!' – I remind them that the long-term strategy for every account is not to blow through the client's money or to think that only large cash outlays can solve a problem. Any company can spend a fortune and beg for more. Wise people put themselves apart by thinking hard to come up with ways to be creative and clever with the resources at hand, and work magic on a tight budget.

One of our brands was keen to be careful with cash and one of our staffers got the bright idea to have baristas sprinkle their logo with chocolate in cappuccinos at their event. People thought it looked so pretty, they posted tons of photos of it on social media, created a viral hashtag, and we wound up getting loads of free coverage. The client was thrilled to be all over Instagram, and it cost them nothing.

Wasting a client's money will never win you their loyalty. In past jobs, I have been in meetings when the client pointedly asked, 'Why did you call such-and-such a person?' or 'Why are we doing this event here and now?' and the account person couldn't clearly and succinctly explain the strategic reasoning behind their decision. Since there wasn't much thought behind it, it's no wonder. 'What's the why?' This question should always be at the forefront of your thoughts.

In any situation, if someone is going to spend their hard-earned money on a service you provide, you had better be able to justify every expense down to the penny with data and wisdom. Having worked with some of the biggest global super-star brands in fashion and beauty, I can tell you that there is no such thing as a smart, canny person randomly throwing money around for no good reason. And you should spend your client's money as if it was your own. Just as the most successful people are details-oriented and will stoop to pick up a piece of rubbish on the shop floor, they are mindful about how their investment will pay off. I don't mean to imply that successful people are frugal per se; rather, they are wise about spending, as we all should be.

Secrecy about Salaries Is a Way to BS Employees

Money is a mysterious aspect of most businesses. It's an unspoken rule that colleagues are not supposed to talk about their salaries and that personal negotiations around salary, bonus and incentives are meant to be confidential. However, systematic secrecy about salaries only serves to keep employees in the dark about whether their salaries are fair and equal. If everyone knew exactly what their colleagues were earning, they'd be aware of discrepancies, despite equal education, experience and performance.

A hallmark of no-BS business is transparency. If a company shrouds salaries in a mysterious shadow, it's a sign that some are being paid more for equal work. We have a very structured remuneration system at TCS whereby we share, openly and transparently, salary brackets based on industry-wide ranges. We can't afford to pay our people what they might make in banking, for example, but within our specific field, our salaries are competitive. If someone gets an offer from another company that we can't beat based on our brackets, we wish them well and let them go. When new people come in, we show them a piece of paper that says what the account managers or directors get paid so they can see the trajectory. Everyone knows, based on the brackets, the range everyone is earning, and that knowledge creates a sense of security and fairness company-wide.

We have taken many ideas from former Waitrose boss Mark Price's book, *Fairness for All*.[6] The John Lewis Partnership has a fascinating model, based on real values and partnership. They don't call their staff 'employees'; they are all 'partners' in the business. Although John Lewis is, like many retailers, finding its feet in the new mobile, digital, e-commerce world, it is still one of the UK's most trusted, loved businesses. I admire Mark a great deal.

The gender pay gap

According to a 2018 survey by the Office for National Statistics, the gender pay gap for hourly earnings in the UK is 8.6 per cent, meaning that, on average, women bring in that percentage less than men.[7] As of 2018, all British companies with 250 or more employees are required to report the median salary of male workers and that of their female counterparts. Of the 10,532 companies reporting in 2018, 77 per cent had a gender pay gap.[*]

---

[*] TCS has fewer than 250 employees, but if we did report, our gender pay gap would be 0 per cent. We have far more female employees than male, and our pay structure is based on position only, not gender, age or any other factor.

The discrepancy is particularly large in banks and in retail companies that cater to a female consumer. For example in 2017/18, Boux Avenue, the lingerie company, paid women on average 74 per cent less than its male employees (they made vast improvements the following year, reducing the gap to 15.6 per cent; well done!). In 2018/19, Sweaty Betty paid its nearly all-female workforce (99 per cent of total employees) 66.6 per cent of the salary given to the tiny cadre of male execs. Some of the other companies with the worst gender pay gap were Apple, Ryanair, J. P. Morgan and the Telegraph Media Group.[8]

In America, where TCS has an office, there is no government mandate to release salary figures for mid- and large-sized companies. Only a public flogging will turn the tide on unfair remuneration based on gender. Nike, the world's largest sports footwear and clothing company, which employs 74,000 workers worldwide, went through a seismic shake-up in 2018, spurred by a women-led internal investigation of how female employees were ignored, harassed and stymied there. Eleven offending execs were purged, and CEO Mark Parker declared that a cultural change at Nike was underway so that all employees 'feel included and empowered', as he put it in a company-wide memo.[9] He stuck to his word by launching a comprehensive review of its remuneration and management training programmes to correct past mistakes and encourage equal pay for women and minorities. More than 7000 Nike employees got pay rises thanks to this initiative. As encouraging as this story is, it never would have happened in the first place if the inequality hadn't been made public by the women who'd been affected by it.

The income pay gap

In 2019, Abigail Disney, the great-niece of Walt Disney, publicly decried the $65.6 million salary of Disney CEO Bob Iger as 'insane'. 'No one on the freaking planet is worth that kind of money,' she said. His salary is 1424 times that of the median pay of Disney workers. 'They say [the company] pay[s] more than the federal minimum wage. But they know [$15 an hour] is not a living wage in Anaheim,' she said of Disneyland's Californian hometown. It's been reported that low wages forced some employees to sleep in their cars.[10] Disney is calling for a higher tax on the super-rich to close the income pay gap between CEOs and top-level execs and the rank-and-file workers.

In the US, S&P 500 companies have been required to release data on the income pay gap since 2018. The information has been startling and highlights just how pernicious income inequality is in the West. McDonald's CEO Steve Easterbrook earned $21.8 million in 2017, while the average worker earned less than $8000 – a ratio of 3101 to 1. At retail behemoth Walmart, the 2018 ratio between the average worker's salary ($19,177) and CEO Doug McMillon's ($22.8 million) was 1188 to 1.[11] On a purely emotional level, it just feels wrong.

One might think that the income gap at online retailer Amazon would be stratospheric. Founder and CEO Jeff Bezos is the richest man in the world, after all. His post-divorce $100 billion net worth (give or take a billion) comes from owning 16.3 per cent of his company, but not from his salary.[12] His salary in 2018, including the cost of his personal security, was $1.7

million. Since the average worker earned $28,446, the income ratio was only 59 to 1.

Some US companies pointedly keep that ratio down, including Berkshire Hathaway, the finance firm run by financier Warren Buffett. Buffett has drawn the same salary of $100,000 for the last thirty years. The average worker salary in 2018 was $53,510, a ratio of less than 2 to 1. Buffett's relatively small salary is largely symbolic. His estimated $86 billion net worth comes from owning sixty companies.[13] He famously lives frugally and has a social conscience. Buffett, along with Microsoft founder Bill Gates and Melinda Gates (net worth: $92 billion) created The Giving Pledge, an organization for high-net-worth individuals to give half of their fortunes to philanthropic projects around the world. So far, $600 billion has been pledged.

In the UK, we need to keep an eye on the CEO-to-worker income gap as well. A 2018 'Fat Cat' study estimated that it takes a CEO three days to earn what the average worker will make in a year.[14] The highest income gap ratio in 2017 was housebuilding company Persimmons. CEO Jeff Fairburn received £47.1 million in pay, a ratio of 1130 to 1 compared to the average worker. In 2018, despite the company receiving the lowest customer satisfaction rating for Home Builders Federation's annual survey, Fairburn received the biggest CEO bonus in the country of £75 million, which caused something of a furore about the excesses of executive pay. The increase in share price, a huge windfall for the company and its top executives, was due to a government scheme to help new homebuyers get interest-free loans. So, in effect, Persimmon's great year and Fairburn's bonus were funded by UK taxpayers. To the average worker earning £29,000, the whole affair was offensive and, bowing to public outcry, Fairburn left his position in November 2018, and then failed to set up a promised charity that might have helped his image problem.[15]

Hopefully, the series of scandals and the public outcry will force companies to justify their remuneration packages from top to bottom. The more transparency the better, I say. Not only are open books ethical, they are forcing change – often via a necessary dose of shame – throughout the business world. Workers should be adequately compensated and valued for their labour. Fair pay for all isn't only a quality of life issue for the individual. Income inequality and wage stagnation are bad for national economies, due to low consumer spending, too much debt and slow growth. Forcing companies to lift their kimonos (as it were) could lead to change that will be good for everyone. Now is the time in the history of corporate finance – owing to the democracy of digital media and government initiatives – to demand fair pay.

Incentivize Profits

What does any employee need and want from an employer? To be paid reliably what they deserve. Granted, many BS companies do this. But I wonder if unethical bosses would withhold their own salaries to pay their staff? During rough patches at TCS, my partner and I did not draw a salary at all. In the early months of starting the company, I always paid the staff salaries before my own. Some months, there was nothing left in the pot for me. It was tough, but it was the right thing to do.

As for bonus incentives, our scheme was designed so that people on the senior level are interested and motivated to think about the business's success overall, not just the success of their particular department. In some years, one arm of the business might far outperform another. Say fashion smashes it and makes a huge profit, that doesn't mean that beauty and lifestyle are penalized. Our bonus scheme for junior staffers is performance-related. At the discretion of their direct leaders, juniors whose work truly stands out are given an unfixed, appropriate amount.

Our philosophy for remuneration is 'all carrot, no stick'. In most BS companies, competition, not cooperation, is encouraged, so you have situations where one director tries to steal a client from another or even sabotages a colleague's work to make herself look good in comparison, which is a stereotypically 'male', winner-takes-all mindset. We subscribe to the one-for-all-and-all-for-one 'female' approach. One of the major topics of discussion in our weekly Working Together leadership meetings is how to divide the revenues for a crossover account fairly between departments, and how to navigate servicing those accounts with multiple teams. It is not easy, and it does cause problems. In this instance, I work hard with people to think of serving the client first, not how much money they are going to get into their part of the P&L. There are leaders at TCS who get this, and others who struggle with it.

Our leadership profit-sharing scheme is organized in three circles – we call them bonus balls! Each circle determines one-third of their bonus. The first circle is how well the company did as a whole. This has proven to be excellent motivation for, say, a fashion director to steer new business towards beauty, or beauty to pitch in on lifestyle accounts. The second circle is the P&L breakdown for each different department. The last circle is about culture and values. If a leader has achieved incredible P&L numbers that exceeded every target, but was not culturally on point, their bonus will reflect that. On the other hand, if a leader hasn't hit their targets, but has exemplified our culture and values like a champ, their bonus will get a boost.

You may think that measuring culture and values is an impossible task, but in fact it is measured (almost) as objectively as a P&L statement. For example, we base it on the results of *The Sunday Times* Best Small 100 Companies employee survey, where all the staff anonymously rate office morale and leadership. We use the data we compile from that survey, as well as anecdotal reports and observations from the teams, to reach fair conclusions about how well people live up to our no-BS ideals. Before appraisals, we ask all those who work with this person (*not* just the senior staff) what they are like to work for, whether they have expressed the company values of strength, passion, care and wisdom, and whether their team has been nurtured, supported and looked after.

Incentivizing good behaviour is no guarantee that people won't behave like idiots sometimes, but when employees know that a meaningful part of their annual salary is based on being a decent human being, they'll be more likely to pause and take that extra breath before reacting when angry or upset. Less drama means greater productivity. Team members will probably check-in more closely with the emotional temperature in the office, and remedy it if needed. Patience and compassion grow leadership skills and quickly put the spotlight on those with the real talent to get to the top.

Benefits Should be Family-Friendly and Emotionally Generous

Benefits are part of the overall remuneration package, and give smaller companies a way to compete if they aren't able to pay higher salaries. A comprehensive and highly competitive benefits package should match up with a company's core values. For example, a health food company ought to offer its people nutritious meals or cooking classes. If a company sells products for women, or has a mostly female customer base, it should offer benefits that are helpful to its female employees. A brand that sells pregnancy products had better have a fantastic maternity leave policy. Not only is the company practising what it preaches, it's also training people to be better advocates for the brand.

Our core values include care and strength (of body and mind), and we demonstrate these by trying to look after TCS staffers' physical and mental health and well-being. Along with medical care for employees, we give people compassionate leave to care for ill or impaired loved ones. Allowing our people to take time off when they are in crisis is how we show that we care. Our staff is predominantly female and, on any given year, we could have five employees at home with their newborns. I would like to think we look after our mothers well – our maternity leave policy further enhances what the government requires for a small business. I remember being shocked to learn from a friend who worked for one of the biggest newspaper groups that, when she went back to work after the legal maternity leave period, she was demoted and told that no allowances would be made for her just because she was a mum. Our philosophy is the complete opposite. We make it as pleasant as possible to return to work, starting with a system called 'Back to Work Days', to smoothly transition from leave into work mode. We give our staff flexible hours. Some mums arrive early and leave early so they have extra time with their kids. Some of our staffers negotiate a nine-day fortnight schedule to have two days at home. Whenever possible, we try to accommodate part-time schedules for parents.

We do our best by new parents, and I'm actually quite proud of the work we do, and by how many of them come back after having babies. Quite often people are much better at their jobs having become parents. They are more mature and considerate and can see things in the round. Because they have to! Other times, becoming a parent is so all-consuming for a person that they can't fully focus on work. Their minds (and hearts) have moved on: it just depends on the person.

Any benefits package should be useful to cure whatever issues the job itself might create. Given how competitive the business world can be, it'd be a good idea to provide burned-out employees with a way to relieve stress and address emotional or mental health problems. No matter what a BS corporate culture might believe, stress, anxiety and burnout are not fixed by ignoring them and hoping they just go away, or by having a stiff drink.

We have a programme in place (which was suggested by one of our leaders, Fiona Hemming), to help anyone who needs support to find it and pay for it. In our history, there have been a couple of extreme cases – two young women (no longer with the company) who were clearly not eating well. We followed all legal protocols for intervention and had a chat with them about it. Both admitted that they were struggling. We were able to co-fund psychotherapy for both of them and helped them through it. I'm delighted to say that they're now living happy, healthy lives. We have since partnered with the mental health charity Mind. They come in and do workshops on topics such as stress relief, life skills and how to spot warning signs for emotional problems in others. They also have anonymous hotlines if people prefer private talks to group discussion or workshops. Mind is available to all of our employees, and our relationship with this charity puts some of my anxiety about the wellness of our people to rest.

Little Extras Matter

Over and above one's salary and benefits, a no-BS company can find other ways to show appreciation to employees with non-monetary perks that enrich their time at the office. Just providing them with a nice place to work and basic comforts – a comfortable workspace, well-maintained equipment and great snacks – is a good start. If possible, value employees by giving them even more so that they're happy to come to the office and enjoy the experience of being there. In our London office, we have a great café, which, at the beginning, was run by an amazing Nigerian lady called Comfort, who nourished employees with healthy, hearty and delicious smoothies, teas, coffees and lemon waters. Now, Marcia, who has taken over, is equally warm and giving, each and every day. We've had wellness specialists, yoga classes and office parties, too.

A publishing company can give its employees free books, and they will, in turn, talk about them to other readers. A retailer offers employees discounts on clothing, and they will show them off to whomever they meet. A company should give to its workers whatever it can to make them feel like an integral part of it. We represent many beauty brands, and our people are lucky enough to try plenty of products as well. Not only do they benefit from excellent skincare information, but they are also walking advertisements for the brands. Nothing makes a client feel happier than seeing their products being used well by real people – everyone's happy.

It might seem counter-intuitive to offer perks that take people away from the office, but a no-BS company has to acknowledge that we're all humans who have lives outside of work, too. It's fairly standard for people to get a day off for their birthday, extra holiday between Christmas and New Year, and summer hours where everybody goes home at 3 p.m. on Fridays. We do all that at TCS, plus we're trying to work out a new policy that I'm really excited about: a sabbatical programme whereby after every five years of service, you could get one month of paid leave to do something that is meaningful to you that falls within the company's values of passion, care, strength and wisdom, and ideally has a philanthropic or charitable bent. So, if a veteran staffer wants to meditate in Bhutan for a month, we will continue to pay her salary as long as she throws in some community service as well.

If a company wants to attract talent and keep employees happy, they should do whatever they can, and then a little bit more. It's just good business. Giving someone a day off, smoothies and yoga is a lot more cost-effective than retraining a new employee.

You Can't Have Too Many Senior People

In hierarchical BS offices, employees are often promoted only if a slot above them opens up. Because of pyramid structures, there are fewer and fewer opportunities for people to advance as they move up the corporate ladder. What happens is that those at the top hang on to their jobs for dear life, and those in the middle get stuck and grow resentful and jealous. It's no wonder that a cutthroat 'whatever it takes' mentality comes into play in such offices.

We do things differently. One value that we strive to reinforce at TCS is recognition. We want our people to know that we appreciate them and applaud their achievements. To show them how much we mean it, we wind up promoting and giving pay rises quite often. Twice yearly, we have an appraisal period for all employees. In July, we do a two-hour formal process where we sit down and talk about values and objectives. Each employee can express how they have embodied the values of strength, wisdom, passion and care in the previous six months. We go over the objectives they defined in that appraisal, and how they have or haven't achieved their goals, whether they feel like they've fallen short or gone above and beyond, and the reasons behind it. We meet again around Christmas for a shorter check-in about how they are feeling and whether there's anything they'd like to discuss.

These appraisals are very much a two-way conversation, emotionally based, and a safe place to talk about minor gripes, to celebrate triumphs and to ask for whatever they might want. Often, people come in and say, 'I've been an account manager for a year and a half, and I'm bored. I'd like a promotion to director.'

In that capacity, we'd take out the policy book, look at the job descriptions of an account manager and account director, and see what they have to do to get there, breaking it down into six objectives for the next six months. If the person comes back in six months and has achieved all of the objectives, they get a promotion. Sometimes it might take longer, but most people who set out to advance get there eventually.

Promoting from within keeps people happy, and clients also have continuity and accountability. Since the next jump is only ever six objectives away, people stay motivated without the stress of hitting a ceiling. We can promote with impunity because we have a horizontal structure, not a pyramid. At the moment, on one team that's worth about £2.7 million, we've got two senior directors. If we had three of them, they could do even more. More senior directors mean more clients and more business, for the benefit of everyone. Having too many talented, committed, seasoned senior people should be the worst problem we ever have.

The way I see it, a company is like a tree, with the senior people being the roots underneath, the middle people as the branches and the assistants and interns as the bright green leaves. The duties and responsibilities of the root people are to be the foundational strength beneath everyone else, to allow the branches and leaves to be the best they can possibly be, so why not have many deep, sturdy roots? At TCS, we're all about sturdy roots and spreading new seeds so the tree of our company can grow. I have an illustration of this tree. It really does turn business hierarchy on its head where endless PowerPoints show the chairman and CEO at the very top. No, at TCS, Daniel, myself and the leadership team are all listed right at the bottom of the page, as the roots supporting the growing, younger teams to be the best and most beautiful they can be.

If someone reaches the figurative top of their team or department, why not ask them to go out there and find something new and lead that? There are always new pathways to create, new areas of business to pursue and explore. There should be no ceiling at TCS, glass or otherwise. Our people are given the freedom to look for opportunities and go after them, and I'm more than happy to celebrate them for a job well done.

Sometimes it doesn't work out and, if so, we'll do all we can to help that person find another job that works better for them. There have been times when we've lost incredible talent because the talent was growing more quickly than TCS.

THE TWO GREATEST ASSETS YOU'LL EVER HAVE

Your true wealth is not measured in pounds, dollars or any monetary currency. Your greatest assets are your reputation and your relationships. With a reputation for being smart, determined and reliable, you'll be a pleasure to work with and make friends with colleagues and clients wherever you go. With a large network of people who adore you, you'll always be a magnet for opportunity.

MONEY

Wealth can be measured in dollars *and* sense. An ethical company values people *and* profit. Making money is fantastic, but a compassionate company gives it back to those who helped bring it in.

- Unscrupulous short-term profit-taking causes long-term and far-reaching damage. Duh!
- Simplify accounts by keeping them straightforward and transparent. Being honest about finances will keep you out of prison and prevent a nervous breakdown.
- Budgets are guidelines, and are not set in stone. You can't anticipate every expense, so be flexible and have some reserves to fall back on if you go over.
- Lean years happen and are nothing to be ashamed of or to hide from. If you can explain what happened and how you adjusted, you'll look strong, not weak.

- If the client or the account is horrible to work with, no fee is worth it.
- Don't take every offer that comes your way if the quantity affects the quality. Make a little less and keep up standards.
- Charge what you're worth and go the extra mile. If someone baulks at your fee, you can back it up with results.
- If someone is overpaying you, reduce the fee. Your fairness will be repaid to you in one way or another.
- Talk about salary brackets to close pay gaps.
- Bosses: shower your people with love, care, good pay, benefits and perks. Show your appreciation and they will work hard.

6 Recruitment

In 2019, a Virginia-based tech recruiting firm called Cynet Systems was caught in a very uncomfortable situation. It posted an account manager job on LinkedIn for a tech job in Florida with a highly specific requirement. Potential candidates, according to the listing, would be 'preferably Caucasian'. Naturally, Twitter users took the recruiting firm to task for the blatantly discriminatory ad. The irony is that Cynet's co-CEO Ashwani Mayur, and the co-owner, are both Indian-American and 60 per cent or their workers are people of colour. Mayur issued an apology, saying, the ad 'does not reflect our core values of inclusivity & equality... We understand why some may have been upset seeing this listing, because we were, too.'[1] The employee who wrote and posted the ad was fired.

It was the second time Cynet posted a questionable ad. A previous one called for 'female candidates only'. Although women in tech are underrepresented, any ad that asks for members of only one demographic group is inherently discriminatory. Regarding both ads, both Cynet and LinkedIn deleted them as soon as they became aware and have vowed to review job postings with even greater scrutiny in the future.[2]

I don't doubt that Mayur was honestly appalled that those ads found their way online with his company's name attached, and his taking decisive action to condemn it was the right thing to do. In admirable no-BS style, he admitted a mistake and took immediate steps to ensure it wouldn't happen again.

Discrimination is recruitment's number one BS issue. It might be as blatant as posting a job for 'preferably Caucasian' candidates, but companies can also be a lot sneakier about how they eliminate candidates based on race, sex and education.

In 2015, one study looked at the hiring practices of elite British companies in the fields of law, finance and accounting – cumulatively, they hold 45,000 of the best jobs in the UK – and found that these companies screened candidates based on their accents, mannerisms and, not surprisingly, the poshness of the school, college or university they went to.[3] Seventy per cent of the top jobs went to the 11 per cent of the population that attended selective schools, leaving even talented working-class applicants with fewer upper level prospects.

Facebook was taken to task in 2019 by anti-discrimination watchdog groups for allowing companies to target job ads to specific demographic groups, like people under forty, and wound up settling a lawsuit over this issue for $5 million and vowing to change their ways. According to *The New York Times*, Sheryl Sandberg, Facebook COO, said, 'We think this settlement is historic and will go a long way toward making sure that these types of discriminatory practices can't happen' after allowing them to happen for quite some time.[4]

In an ideal no-BS world, a qualified person would be able to see all the job listings that fit their skills and experience. But that is not always possible. In 2015, American big box retail department store Target was fine $2.8 million by the Equal Employment Opportunities Commission (EEOC) for having thousands of candidates fill out assessment tests – interpreted by psychologists – that screened out black, Asian, female and disabled would-be workers for mid-level jobs. 'The [hiring] tests were not sufficiently job-related and consistent with business necessity, and thus violated Title VII of the Civil Rights Act of 1964' the statement for the EEOC reads.[5] To its credit, Target reacted by changing its hiring process and being ever-vigilant about discriminatory practices creeping back in.

Diversity Means Profitability

In the UK, the law prohibits discrimination. Hiring managers should not even know the name of the candidates, let alone their gender, age or ethnicity. New legislation goes further to protect people's personal data and I'm glad about it. As a nation, we have a significant problem with diversity, especially at the top. I am investigating an online platform that allows a huge part of the initial interview process to be anonymous, screening out a candidate's name, age, gender and racial identity.

Dame 'Steve' Shirley (one of the first female tech icons who built a software company in the 1970s) told a brilliant story at the Founders Forum in 2018, which I was fortunate enough to attend. Back in the mid-1950s, she wrote lots of letters to companies selling her services signed with her real name, Stephanie Shirley. She never got a job. Over supper with her husband one night, he said, 'You should change your name to Steve and see what happens.' The rest is history and Dame Vera Stephanie 'Steve' Shirley is one of the most impressive people you'll ever meet. Let's hope the world's cultural biases will change to ensure that all those with the talent, will to work and desire can come to the table (or the labs) as equals.

According to a 2017 study, only 6 per cent of management positions in FTSE 100 companies are held by black, Asian and minority ethnics (BAME).[6] It's probably fewer than 6 per cent actually, because only 21 per cent of those companies publish diversity stats. Only 54 per cent 'champion BAME diversity' and 15 per cent are committed to change.[7] Hence, the tiny number of BAME in top companies is unlikely to increase anytime soon.

In 2016, Sir John Parker, chairman of Anglo American, a mining giant, put forward in the Parker Review the recommendation that, by 2021, FTSE 100 companies must have a person of colour as a director; by 2014, FTSE 250 companies should do the same. Progress is slow or non-existent. Below are the key findings in executive search and consult firm Green Park's 2018 leadership survey of the 10,000 top jobs at those firms:[8]

- White executives hold 96.7 per cent of 'top three' roles in FTSE 100 companies.
- 3.3 per cent are held by BAME leaders.
- There are five BAME CEOs and three BAME CFOs of FTSE 100 companies, both increasing by one from the previous year.
- The number of BAME Chairs has fallen from three to two.

- The number of BAME non-executive directors has reached double digits for the first time.
- Following a substantial rise in 2017, from 5.7 per cent to 10.7 per cent, the Top 100 positions held by people of colour has declined to 10.6 per cent.

At TCS, we are diverse. One in five staffers is an ethnic minority, and we are always working to increase that number. Our industry is predominantly female, and our staff reflects that; over 80 per cent of us are women. Not only is it ethical and right to have a diverse staff, it's profitable, too. McKinsey & Co., one of the world's most prestigious corporate consultancies, researched the diversity of 1000 companies in twelve countries.[9] The companies that ranked in the top 25 per cent for BAME diversity were 33 per cent more likely to be profitable than those in the lowest 25 per cent. When management was diverse, the impact on performance and profitability was even more dramatic; the companies with the lowest diversity in executive teams were 30 per cent more likely to falter. This correlation was especially relevant in the UK companies.

There has been similar government pressure on UK companies to get more women on their boards as well. Gender diversity is nearly as impactful to a company's success as ethnicity. According to Green Park's survey, the firms with women in management roles were 21 per cent more likely to be profitable. The one area of concern at TCS is that since our company is 90 per cent female, we have our work cut out for us to be more inclusive of men. Inclusion at all levels is a positive and necessary progression, culturally and morally. Anyone who doesn't understand that fact is living in the past and needs to open their eyes to the world we inhabit now.

One last point: the BS business model of money – 'winner takes all', 'whatever it takes' and 'give the least and take the most' – is outdated and will make it harder for companies to recruit diverse and talented newcomers. I asked a huge global drinks company CEO what kept her awake at night, and she told me that her biggest worry is her inability to recruit good talent. Top graduates out of the best schools don't want to work hard for a dinosaur corporation that exists just to make money for shareholders. It's not interesting or fulfilling, and it's not world-changing. There has to be a greater meaning behind what they do for money. I hope and pray that the younger generations never lose their idealism and can be a force for positive change, demanding that they won't work for companies that put profits over people and the planet.

It's Never Too Late to Start Up

Some of the most inspirational woman in business I know found their greatest success later in life. They never thought that, after the age of fifty or sixty, that it was time to sit in a rocking chair and knit all day. Retirement? Why? Nothing's going to slow down women like my friend, former *Vogue* editor Kathy Phillips, who founded her own skincare line, or Sue Harmsworth, who sold her skincare company and is as busy as ever in her advocacy work. Sylvie Chantecaille is also a true inspiration to me. Sylvie is a global entrepreneur. Her eponymous skincare brand is huge.

She has made extraordinary progress in her and her family's passion for animal and habitat conservation, and intertwines this philanthropy seamlessly with the growth and success of the brand. She is a powerful, gentle, beautiful businesswoman, mother, wife, entrepreneur and visionary.

These women are the rare exceptions to the unfortunate trend of older women becoming invisible in the workplace. In the digital age, it's hard for anyone over thirty-five to land a job at a tech company, except for the one token grey-hair roaming the halls – probably not a woman.

I find it so funny that a young person with no proven track record who looks about twelve and wears Converse and ripped jeans can get a decent job in a tech firm or have investors throw money at them to start one up. But a woman with decades of experience in business doesn't usually stand a chance.

The disappearing mature woman in business reminds me of something my doctor told me about how older females were treated in prehistoric times. In the aeons before hormone replacement therapy and kettle bell workouts, a post-menopausal woman's bones became very brittle, and she gained weight, and couldn't run as fast. She wasn't as sexually alluring either and reproduction was no longer on the cards. As far as her tribe was concerned, it was time for her to say 'bye bye'. So, when a pack of wolves came around, the men would grab the children and the nubile young females, and leave the older, redundant women to be chased and eaten.

I'm afraid we're seeing something similar happen in business lately. For example in the last few years, at powerful media houses, new young editors have come in and swept out all the women over fifty in one fell swoop, allegedly to bring in people with fresh new ideas. (As if a mature woman is suddenly plum out of them.) Thanks to advances in healthcare, many of us will live into our nineties and beyond. So what is a fifty-five-year-old woman who has been fired for being irrelevant supposed to do with all the experience she's accumulated over her thirty-year career? Wisdom should never be squandered.

There are many of us who have transcended the vulnerabilities and insecurities of ageing in the business world and continue to set new goals and reach them. Dame Stephanie 'Steve' Shirley had an entrepreneurial career, launching a series of software and science companies, leading the way for female engineers, and has received scores of honours for her career in technology. And then, after she retired at sixty, she got started with her *second* fantastic career in philanthropy in medical research (in particular, for autism and Asperger's syndrome), science and technology. In 2013, at eighty years old, she was named by the BBC as one of Britain's '100 Most Powerful Women'. I don't think there is anything that could stop her. She can show us all a thing or a hundred.

I am all for change in the workplace. The old-fashioned model of the Rupert Murdoch-type CEO lording over minions from a glass-walled corner office is broken. The digital tech world – where most of the good jobs are now and in the future – is native to Millennials and Generation Z. They have lived their lives online from birth in a way that Gen X and Boomers haven't, and they have an enormous amount to teach us. But I believe the best way forward in any company is to take the innovation and energy of youth and combine it with the wisdom and experience of age. That said, the grey-hairs shouldn't sit in a conference room, pontificating about the good ol' days while the young people glance sideways at each other. That will not help them come off as relevant.

Journalist Camilla Cavendish researched changing demographic (soon, there will be more over-sixty-fives than under-fives in the UK) and increasing life expectancy and asked, in her book *Extra Time*, what the 'Young-Old' – healthy and active sixty- and seventy-year-olds – are going to do with the ten, twenty or thirty years they have after traditional retirement age. Perhaps, as she suggests, the answer is not retiring at all, to remain purposeful and useful. As she discovered, many Young-Old Brits are 'un-retiring' to go back to work, or trying to. As Cavendish wrote in *The Telegraph*:

Many employers are reluctant to hire or train people over 50, assuming they are dull plodders. But experiments have suggested that's not true. When the car company BMW put skilled workers over 50 onto one of its production lines, and provided working aids like better lighting and protection from static electricity, the results were astonishing. The older team worked faster than the younger one it had replaced. Productivity grew by seven per cent. Absenteeism dropped from seven per cent to two per cent, below the factory average. And the number of assembly defects fell to zero.[10]

NEVER GIVE UP ON MEANINGFUL WORK

The key to staying young and feeling relevant is by facing new challenges and taking on new opportunities. For women who have been forced out of one company or profession, they might have to start all over again somewhere else. It might seem like a big step down – and it might be – but getting a fresh start does have its advantages. You get to reinvent yourself, learn new skills and meet new people. You have no idea where your life is going to take you, so be open to the possibilities. There does seem to be a cliff that women have to be pushed off to reach their next chapter. You might not be happy about it, but having taken one fall doesn't mean you are redundant in the workplace. You have skills and wisdom to offer. So whenever doubt creeps in, as it does, please repeat to yourself one of my favourite sayings: 'What I need will come, and what will come is what I need.' And then do the best you can.

It's All About Fit

Self-awareness is essential at TCS, and so is other-awareness, otherwise called 'emotional intelligence'. We need to know a lot about each other's individual strengths and how they will enhance the greater good. For example, via our personality/ values assessment tools, I have learned that I'm at my best when I'm untethered and I can take an idea methodically from A to

Z. I guess some people call it flow. When I'm in a presentation and I'm in the zone, my colleagues and team know to just let me go until I'm done. (All the while, though, I am watching them for body language. I know when it's going okay by how they are moving, breathing, reacting.) When I'm confident from reading them that things are going well, I keep going. Then, the people with the top strength of analysis can jump in to pull out my five or six main points to reinforce to the client. If I read that the room is zoning out, not really engaged, I pull back or stop altogether and say honestly that I feel that my presentation is not landing the way that I had hoped, and could I get some feedback.

We need the stream of consciousness types *and* the bullet pointers. So, we don't have a cookie-cutter template for personality, skill set and communications style. We couldn't be a modern business if we only hired, say, extroverts who want to put on parties and do social media blasts for our brands. We're mindful of diversity in character traits as well as areas of expertise.

When recruiting, anyone in management and HR needs to think about diversity in a global sense. An office should feel like a microcosm of the entire world in terms of ethnicities, genders, ages – and gifts. Offices need out-front and back office people. They need creatives and admins. It's all about diverse people with different skills and talents coming together to create a great team.

It's very rare that someone accidentally winds up working at TCS and has to shoehorn themselves into our culture. From the outset, we present ourselves as a collaborative company:

we work and learn together. All the players on the team must have the same set of rules and expectations. A while back, The Daily Telegraph Business Club invited us to take part in a short video series for their digital platform about how we do business.* We shot some scenes around the office, people at their desks, in meetings; Tom and I sat for interview segments about our work philosophy of going back to basics and doing everything with the utmost care, no matter how small. We had to invest a little in the film, but that opportunity paid off times a hundred. The endorsement of a national newspaper, their growing platform and the ensuing PR that we got has been invaluable. Just as importantly, we had a video that defined our culture. Everyone who came to TCS for an interview had watched that video and had immediately 'got' what we were about. They'd only show up for the interview if they felt our culture mirrored theirs. Our candidates are a self-selective group.

Along with a candidate fitting into our culture, our recruitment team screens candidates using a variety of metrics – education, experience, skills, etc. – but the backbone of what we're looking for is a rigorous work ethic and a collaborative spirit. We have created an online survey of questions called the 'Values Way' that helps us sort through a candidate's personal priorities. What do they care deeply about? What motivates and drives them? Do they have passion, strength, wisdom, humility, a caring nature? What traits come out when they're under

---

* To watch the video, go to: https://www.telegraph.co.uk/finance/businessclub/business-club-video/marketing-and-communications-se/8061088/The-Communications-Store.html

pressure? What energy do they put out – or don't put out? What do they love? What do they hate? What is their nature? Who are they? What do they like and dislike so much? In this way, we know each other better in a more structured way. So, when working with someone, this allows us to say, 'Okay, I know how x is going to react to this, because this makes x feel uneasy and uncomfortable. I won't put x in that situation, but I can find y who loves this kind of thing.'

Don't Force Candidates to Jump Through Hoops

If a candidate isn't pre-screened via unfair assessment tools and/ or targeted ads and has managed to apply for a position that matches their skills and experience, they're really just getting started. And there might be big BS hurdles yet to clear.

A friend of mine told me this story about her job quest as an events coordinator for a marketing firm:

I was told that over a hundred people applied for the job, and that the computer program they used to screen CVs put mine in the top ten for the job. I was thrilled to hear it. To get to the next round – an interview with the head of marketing at the company – I was asked to write three separate pitches for three of their current clients. The HR person I spoke to confided to me that competition was stiff, and that if I wanted to make it to the next round, my pitches had to really stand out.

I'd been freelancing for a while and had written dozens of marketing pitches in my time. A good pitch usually takes at least ten hours to research and write. To do the three they asked for, I'd have to put in thirty hours of free work. If I were to bill directly to a client, I'd charge thousands for this much effort. It seemed like a lot to ask but I really wanted this job and did my very best. I submitted three excellent pitches and waited for a response. A week went by. Two weeks. Three weeks. Finally, after a month of sending 'checking in' emails, I heard from the HR person that I didn't get the job. I was disappointed and a bit bitter about it, but I soldiered on and landed a position at another company.

A few months went by, and then I ran into a friend of mine at a party who worked at one of the companies the marketing firm represented. I'd mentioned to her that I'd had to write an extensive marketing pitch for one of their new products and described some key points. She told me that my ideas were actually the ones they were currently using. I can't prove it, and I don't dare make a big deal of it, but I think that marketing firm used my pitch as their own. Essentially, they got a week's work out of me for free, and then didn't even hire me!

When considering what hiring practices seem fair and which don't, all one can do is use basic instinct and an innate sense of justice. Forcing a candidate to do free work and then using it without compensation or consent is obviously unfair and might even be theft.

Most employers will ask a candidate to provide a sample of work, and there's nothing wrong with that – it's a useful exercise that helps the employer figure out whether a candidate is a good fit. However, if a company requests original work, it shouldn't take longer than two or three hours to complete. Any employer that asks for a full day's work or more might be taking advantage – an important factor to consider before going to work at that company. The 'good fit' assessment goes both ways.

DON'T FIT A SQUARE PEG INTO A BLACK HOLE

If you are a candidate for hire and feel that your values do not mesh with those of your new company, remove yourself quickly so you won't be dragged down or corrupted by it. If you feel you won't be compromised, then you should inject your no-BS values of kindness and compassion into all your personal interactions with your colleagues and clients. Always remember to build on your assets of reputation and relationships. You will need your colleagues at a BS company to write you some references when you leave.

Living up to your personal values will improve your work life on a day-to-day basis even at a 'bad fit' job. But, be warned: in hardcore BS offices, kindness might be perceived as weakness, and people might try to take advantage of you. Don't make the mistake of thinking that kindness disallows you to be tough. Tough, yes; ruthless or aggressive, no.

Day One Tells You Everything You Need to Know

If you have been recruited and officially hired by a company, the first day at your new job will probably be representative of the overall experience of working there. Are people pleasant to be around? Are your responsibilities clearly defined? Have you received a proper welcome? Proper training? Do you know who to ask for guidance?

At TCS, when someone joins us, we try to take care to make them feel included, acknowledged and welcomed. First, their team leader sends out an all-staff email welcoming them, telling us all a little about them, and including their new TCS email address and a picture so we can recognize the new team member around the office. I try to email every single recruit myself in their first week to welcome them and hope that they enjoy their time at TCS. It takes me two minutes.

We also host everyone at what I describe as a 'beginners' breakfast'. It lasts one hour. We serve breakfast and just chat. I usually ask the newbies where they've come from, what their new role is and why they wanted the job. Often, the new recruits have not met one another yet, and so it's a good way to get to know each other and form bonds with some peers as they start out. Then I talk to the group about the company history of why we got started in the first place, our ethos and the four key values of strength, wisdom, passion and care. I lay out some basic codes of conduct and make sure everyone feels appreciated and welcome.

Next, the new person is passed along to their team leader for a comprehensive office tour and more training and guidance about their specific duties. Our HR director, Claire, manages the 'on-boarding' integration process for all new employees. She understands TCS ethos better than any, and she and her team work hard to make sure people are not dropped in it from the word go. Make no mistakes, starting a new job can be terrifying. And, as kind and welcoming as we are, joining TCS is a bit like jumping onto a speeding train. There is so much work to be done and fast, but we do what we can to make sure that anyone who feels overwhelmed has a safety net and a tangible support system.

I tell everyone that if they don't see our values playing out in reality in our workplace, that my door, Daniel's or Claire's are always open to talk about it. And we encourage everyone to ask questions of their colleagues and the leadership team. When people seek information, they are practising our core value of wisdom. If you are just starting a new job, do not hesitate to ask away. Don't worry about looking stupid. You won't come off that way to a reasonable human being. A good boss at every level should never be too busy or too important to answer someone's questions. We should all always be available to help someone out.

Going through the recruitment process is never fun when you are looking for work. But if a company is ethical – doesn't discriminate, doesn't exploit candidates by forcing them to do free work and hires based on values and 'fit' – then it's likely that wherever a candidate winds up, they are in the right place and all those rejections were blessings in disguise. A BS company that would fire a talented worker because they're not white or male or posh or young enough is not a place where a compassionate ethical no-BS person would thrive anyway.

Hit the ground running

No matter how smoothly you're integrated into a company, the most important entry-level tip I can offer is that you must be ready to work. Hard. I don't want anyone to get the impression that just because you've been lucky enough to land at a no-BS office you aren't expected to work really, really hard. Sometimes people make the mistake of thinking that because we are kind and empathetic they can take advantage. Big mistake. The phrase 'give an inch, take a mile' springs to mind. Feeling safe, supported and comfortable must not be misinterpreted as having nothing to push against. What it means is that you don't need to be berated or bullied into hard work. We want self-motivation, rigour, tenacity – and we give thanks and rewards for it.

RECRUITMENT

Finding new talent to fill a job is a job in and of itself. To best survive the ordeal:

- The law is on the side of fairness; if a company discriminates, it can be held accountable.
- Diversity in recruitment leads to profitability. When management comes in all colours, companies thrive.

- A good match between a candidate and a company has to be values-based. It's not enough to be qualified to do the work. Can the candidate fit into the corporate culture and embody the company's values?
- A candidate should be expected to go through the process with enthusiasm. However, if they feel like they're being taken advantage of, they should read that as a sign that the company in question might not be a good fit for them.
- Once a candidate becomes a colleague, the assessment isn't over. The no-BS truth is that workers are always being tested, so work as hard in the job as you did to get it.

7 Start-Ups

S ome start-ups are bound to fail, even if it takes a while before anyone realizes that the company's foundation is total BS.

In 2003, Stanford University student Elizabeth Holmes founded Theranos, a Silicon Valley biotech company. She claimed to have invented a cheaper, more accurate way to carry out blood tests with just a tiny finger prick sample. If her machine worked, it could end the invasive method of venepuncture, get results to patients faster and prevent untold pain and suffering. Early investors flooded Theranos with $400 million, making Elizabeth Holmes a Silicon Valley darling. At its peak, the company was valued to be worth $9 billion. General James Mattis, George Shultz and Henry Kissinger were among the many powerful elites who sat on the company's board or invested heavily. Rupert Murdoch put in $100 million.

The only problem was that the technology Theranos engineers were tasked with building never worked. Through multiple versions, the blood test box that Holmes sold to pharmacy chains and the US military did not do what she said it could do. In fact, according to an exposé in the *Wall Street Journal* in 2015, reporter John Carreyrou stated that, of the 240 types of blood tests Theranos claimed it could do, it could accurately perform only twelve.[1] What's more, it was claimed that government inspectors were given falsified data; the company suspiciously deleted data as well. CEO Holmes and COO Ramesh Balwani – her partner in life and work – perpetuated the deception by producing documents, allegedly authored with pharmaceutical company partners, that were actually written by employees and packed with false or misleading information. In 2016, the US Securities and Exchange Commission charged Holmes with fraud to the tune of $700 million. Balwani was accused of engaging in a scheme to defraud millions from investors and was indicted. In September 2018, the company officially folded, multiple millions in debt, and Holmes and Balwani, at the time of writing, are awaiting trial, maintaining their innocence. Except for the whistle-blowers and journalists who exposed the scandal, everyone associated with the company took a financial blow or was professionally disgraced.

In his book *Bad Blood*[*] John Carreyrou described all the ways that Theranos went wrong.[2] Rushing to market when the tech was not ready. The company culture of secrecy and paranoia. Holmes's refusal to compromise her vision, despite engineers insisting on the impossibility of a table-top-sized box performing hundreds of tests on a single drop of blood. The 'fake it till you make it' philosophy of deceiving investors and partners with the hope that, one day, the lie would be true. Instead of being remembered for changing medical testing, as

---

* Also the subject of an HBO documentary – *The Inventor: Out For Blood in Silicon Valley*, directed by Alex Gibney.

was Holmes's intention, Theranos will always be thought of as an epic failure and an example of how start-ups can go so horribly wrong.

Start with the Best Intentions

Anyone who cares enough about ethical business principles to buy this book might be harbouring the dream of launching a new company. And who among us would object to a would-be CEO forming a new company with the very best of intentions, even with the lofty goals of making the world a better place?

The trouble is when the lofty goal is the sum total of what the founder has to offer. No one could fault Holmes for dreaming big and trying to create her science-fiction-worthy technology, but good intentions alone aren't enough.

According to a report by Enterprise Research Centre, a research firm that tracks small- and medium-sized companies in the UK, only half of the start-ups formed in London in 2013 stayed in business for at least three years.[3] However, those that don't collapse have a decent chance of doing well. Among the still-standing companies in the study, they grew 20 per cent year-on-year during the study period.

As for what makes a new company succeed or fail, there are a whole host of reasons. But according to a 2015 study of all the failed companies in the UK that were founded between 2011 and 2014, more than half went under because of incompetent leadership and mismanagement.[4] The study cited poor or lack of training at the top. People had the enthusiasm for and dream of starting a company but lacked the training and expertise to pull it off.

Theranos's Holmes would fall into this category, although her personal charisma and conviction kept her company going for fifteen years, despite never creating a single viable product.

When I started my business, I had no idea what I was doing. I'd never started a business before. The first thing I did was to acknowledge that I was inexperienced, and to confront the very real possibility of failure. It was my first ethical, compassionate act as the CEO of my start-up: being honest with myself. I was not going to 'fake it till I made it'. I was going to do my best and work myself incredibly hard to make it. Faking it – literal BSing – should never be part of any ethical start-up's business plan.

Pursue Your Passion

True passion is inherently authentic. If an entrepreneur loves whatever they're doing, then they will have the fortitude to keep going despite the many challenges they'll face.

Jo Fairley is one the most extraordinary women I've ever met and is the walking definition of how far you can go if you pursue your passion. She left school at sixteen to get into publishing, landed her first job as a secretary at a magazine and rose steadily from there. At the age of twenty-three, she became the youngest editor-in-chief in England of *Look Now*. As a boss, she was known for giving her staff the freedom to follow their instincts and, as she has said, 'Just have a go!' at whatever projects intrigued them. She applied the same attitude to her diverse interests. Co-author of *The Beauty Bible*, Jo could have carried on in journalism, but another passion intervened – the passion for chocolate. Inspired by a postcard she bought on Carnaby Street in 1991 that read, 'If you don't do it, you'll never know what would have happened if you had,' she invested some savings in two tons of organic dark chocolate that she and her husband Craig Sams (also a genius), who ran Whole Earth Foods, turned into Green & Black's chocolate, the first UK company to earn a fair trade certificate, and now a $100-million brand. Since then, she's founded an organic food store and bakery, a wellness centre and The Perfume Society.

Green & Black's, sourced from farmers in Belize, was the world's first organic chocolate and, for years, Fairley's was the only brand that was selling it. A company that is 'first' and/or 'only' at giving customers something they want (or didn't know they wanted yet) is in a unique, enviable position to succeed. That drive for innovation and originality continues to motivate Fairley. As she told the *Guardian*, 'I really like doing things that nobody else has done before. I am a pioneer – it seems really weird saying it – but many, many businesses that I see have looked at what somebody else has done and decided to copy that. Unless you can create a real point of difference, I don't see the virtue in having a business which is just there to do something somebody else has already done.'[5]

My passion flowed from the idea of creating a workplace like no other I'd seen. I let my imagination guide me as I jotted down ideas and found that my non-committal business plan just flowed effortlessly. I've learned over the years that sometimes, when you set out to do something wholeheartedly, doors just keep opening, and you can keep going through them. One thing leads to another. Other times, plans are made, and a course is carefully plotted, and yet the doors don't open or they slam in your face. Starting up TCS was one of those open-door times.

Another thing that played out in my favour was that I was a complete unknown, and so the stakes were low. No one would be watching and waiting for me to succeed or fail. Being a total nobody can be a very useful, private and safe place to be. As Janis Joplin once sang, 'Freedom's just another word for nothing left to lose.' I had passion, and a plan, and nowhere to fall. I was already at the bottom, which is an excellent place to start one's journey upward.

Have a Clear Vision

Every company begins somewhere, and it's usually in the imagination of its founder. If someone intends to open a shop or restaurant, they should have a vision of the menu and the design vibe. If someone hopes to launch an app, they should know what it's going to do and who the audience for it might be. 'Vision' can mean a lot of different things, but a good way to get a handle on it is simply to close one's eyes and try to see the future business. What will it look like? What will it feel like to be there? Go ahead and dream it up. Embellish the vision as it becomes clearer.

When I started my PR agency at my kitchen table, I had a clear sense of what it would be like to show up for work each morning. My vision was already well defined in my mind, mainly as a reaction to toxic BS office environments I'd seen previously.

My dream workplace would be collaborative, creative, unconventional, full of clever people working with passion and gusto for clients they could be proud to represent, as little hierarchy as possible, no fear and no office politics. The leadership would be a team of equals, the best in the business, each one in charge of their own department. Collectively, they'd be like the spokes on an umbrella. For the company to function, each spoke would be strong and straight. I'd be the spoke for the beauty department, and I'd bring in other directors with specialities in fashion, lifestyle, events, etc. Every client would feel like they were getting top-shelf attention and experience from senior people, even if they didn't work directly with me.

This egalitarian ideal helped me name the company. Some of my friends and early advisors suggested The Dexter Agency and Dexter PR, but naming the company after myself wasn't scalable or, in my mind, a sustainable business formula. By setting myself up as the star of the company and putting my own name over the door, my future clients would only be happy with my attention. If the company grew and I couldn't be the point of contact for every client, they might feel pawned off on junior accounts people, a phenomenon I'd seen time and time again. Even when my company was just me, I never envisioned I'd be alone for long and so I chose an honest name that spoke of my intentions: The Communications Store.

As far as a vision of the actual office, I was sometimes not brave enough to imagine it. In my short career to date, I'd been in the chicest offices but none of those places made me feel comfortable or that I belonged. I wanted our office to be inclusive, relaxed, unfrightening. A place where someone would just smile at you, make you feel welcome, offer you a cup of coffee, not sashay around in stilettoes and a pencil skirt looking outwardly powerful, important and unapproachable. In the service business, it's not about the fancy office, it's about the people.

Know the Reason for Being

According to CB Insights, a market intelligence consulting firm, 42 per cent of start-ups fail because there is 'no market need' for it.[6] The reason Green & Black's quickly found its products on supermarket shelves across the world was because it identified a market need for really excellent, organic, fair trade dark, chocolate.

Beyond good intentions and passion, market need must be motivating a start-up's founding if it has any shot at surviving long-term. Often, people want to launch a company very quickly, to meet a fleeting demand. The thought process I've heard goes something like, 'I'll start an app or cook up a hair mask and make billions!' But there are already a multitude of hair products and apps out there. What's so special about a new one?

One of the first products my company worked on with John Frieda began with the nightmare that many women on this planet were living with – frizzy hair. John and his business partner Gail wanted to help, and created Frizz Ease, the first silicon serum that really did tame frizz with just a couple of drops applied to damp hair. They put it in a small bottle, charged a reasonable amount and sold it mass-market in pharmacies. Frizz Ease was a fabulous success from inception, and it changed the future of haircare, creating a whole new category. There is a clear dividing line between life before and life after (if you don't believe me, watch any movie before 1997 and just look at the hair), and the line of Frizz Ease products continues to sell briskly to this day. John and Gail's product had a 'reason for being' and was accessible to anyone. It was easy to get wholeheartedly behind this product because the world needed it! It would have been a tougher sell if there were dozens more just like it, or if it didn't work or offered something that people weren't convinced they wanted.

Have a Grand Objective

Besides making money, what is the goal of the company? What does the CEO hope to accomplish? What will the business do better than any other? A future restaurateur's mission might be 'to serve the best fish and chips in town'. A new media company's mission might be 'to generate compelling content that informs and entertains'. A charitable organization's objective might be 'to raise awareness about global poverty' or 'advocate for human rights'. When conceiving an uber-goal, a future CEO should keep it succinct. A grand objective doesn't have to be grandiose. The simpler, the better, in fact.

The original grand objective of TCS was quite humble actually: 'to service clients really well'. My personal mission was to 'work hard, do good, stay humble'. The goal was not to get rich quick or anything other than just signing up some clients (already a big ask), keeping them through sheer hard work, and paying salaries to myself and my future employees. I'd formulated specific mini-goals for how we'd behave in anything and everything we said and did, aka the 'Cs of communication': clever, considered, considerate, clear, clean and, perhaps, counter-cultural in all that we did. I made more lists of goals in other areas, like community involvement, customer satisfaction, recruitment and training, and workspace improvements, to mention a few.

The 'work hard' part

I loved the jotting down of ideas part of starting my business, but nothing would have happened if I hadn't taken care of the practical tasks and made spreadsheets about specific financial benchmarks (how much the company will earn in year one, year two, etc.) with realistic objectives for reaching them.

As an organizational thinker, I enjoyed this part of the process, even though it was hard and painstaking. In a week, I made a month's worth of daily to-do lists of what I was sure I could get done, and then a few more items I thought I could do on top, and some financial breakdowns and projections that I would soon learn bore no resemblance to reality. Accuracy didn't really matter at that point. What did count was having an agenda. I'm the kind of person who is most comfortable when I know what I need to do next. My to-do lists felt like a realistic and achievable call to action. I remember thinking, 'This really could work.'

REFINEMENT

It's one thing to make plans. It's quite another to implement them consistently, on schedule and with excellence.

Very early on, I realized it was not possible to complete everything on my to-do lists. Feeling overwhelmed with the enormity of a task is normal, even if you are an organizational machine and you've got all the things you need to do on a piece of paper.

I'd highly recommend doing list refinement. The strategy is simple. Look at the list and pick the four or five key priorities – and forget the rest. Look at deadlines first, and go with the actions that are the biggest priority and have the shortest deadline. People procrastinate and by the time they've finished focusing on a B-list task, it's too late. And remember to become a master at delayed gratification. Do your worst ones first. Always.

Hire the Right People

When I was founding TCS, I did not know of any other PR agency with the 'work hard, do good, stay humble' business model (probably through my own ignorance) and thought its reason for being was to redefine a new kind of communications shop, one that would attract the most precious people in the field in London. Usually finding the right talent is the hardest thing.

When I started up in the late 1990s it was just me. Despite being on my own, my one and only macro strategy in the beginning was to build relationships. Early on, in lieu of pretty much anything else, I reached for the same tools I still use today to get my business going: empathy, compassion, kindness, humility, humour, rigour, hard work, determination and perseverance. I didn't have fancy software or technology. I didn't have an app or a social media platform (in those days, they didn't exist). I had some expertise in PR, but so did hundreds of other young men and women in London. What would stand out from all of the others were my 'soft' skills of connecting with people, and I put them to hard work.

Without networks, my communications agency wasn't worth anything. I needed to start from the very bottom and build a network from nothing. It thrills me to no end that today, despite the endless mobile and social and digital channels, those skills still work hard for us at TCS. We are a company that is comprised of fallible, messy, imperfect human beings. Our clients and brands might be glamorous and glitzy, but they're just people with personalities, weaknesses, strengths and feelings. Most companies carry the baggage of their reputation. For example, Apple's reputation is 'Innovative!' But when you do business with Apple, you don't sit down with 'Innovative!' You'll interact with a person who might be just as intimidated by the company's reputation as you are. TCS's reputation is 'humble and human'. People should expect to feel at ease as soon as they walk through the door and we make sure that they are.

Looking for the humanity in everyone you work with, be it a colleague, a boss or a client, and behaving like an honest-to-goodness human being, will help you establish the essential relationships you will need to build or grow your company. We've all seen countless tech start-ups that have meteoric rises and then crash. One of the reasons they don't last is that they lack an understanding of how important relationships and loyalty are when you are trying to build something that stands the test of time. Perhaps if the company had been founded with a handful of 'adults in the room', these issues might not be coming up? We'll never know. Perhaps someone might have told them to go a little slower and create things, instead of moving fast and breaking them? I'd rather grow slow and strong than out of control.

Maybe that's why it took us twenty years to open an office in America. But I'm doing it, at fifty! The whole endeavour has been like starting over, forcing me to keep that hunger to take on a different market and to work hard to build a positive reputation from a standing start. It's just as exciting as a quarter of a century ago. And I feel very young still, just starting out!

Some CEOs would say, 'Hire people who would be your friends outside the office.' I'd say look for shared values – the simpatico feeling of 'we're on the same page'. Diversity is strength, but having a shared worldview with partners and colleagues makes mutually working towards a company's goals and purpose that much smoother. Attracting good people is a side-benefit of doing all that mental pre-work. Without clarity and passion about the new company's intention, vision and objective, it'd be a tough sell for even the most charismatic CEO to convince talented people to sign up.

I dreamed of one like-minded person to work with from day one. I'd always imagined that Tom Konig-Oppenheimer would be my business partner in TCS. I just had to convince him to leave his current, well-paid job to come and work with me.

Tom enjoyed his job and was well established there, and in the industry. I asked him how much he was earning and said, 'If I can build my company up enough to match your salary, would you consider coming in with me?' He said yes.

Several months later, quite literally on the day that I had raked together enough money from clients to afford his salary, I got off the bus and, coincidentally, Tom was standing with his dog, Bunny, by the bus stop.

I said, 'I need to talk to you. When can we meet?'

He said, 'How about right here, right now?'

We went to the off licence, bought a bottle of wine and went to his little garden. And that was that. Serendipity.

The two of us devoted ourselves to strengthening our relationships with our two clients: a concept store called Green & Pleasant, and an American all-natural cosmetics brand called Kiss My Face. Both were pioneers in their fields and I was honoured, and so grateful, to work with them. BUT – we needed more clients to survive. So, we literally went shopping for them.

At the time, there was a holistic, fair trade, organic supermarket called Planet Organic, run by Johnny Dwek and Renée Elliott. They didn't have any money for PR, so I offered to work for them for next to nothing, £375 per month to be exact. They agreed, and I used that connection to cold call brands they carried and offer my services. (Tom and I owe Johnny and Renée a lot for letting us represent them.)

One of those brands happened to be Dr. Hauschka. Back in 1996 when Dr. Hauschka signed up with TCS, they were turning over a very small amount. The Dr. Hauschka skincare company came out of an interesting philosophical movement with profound values, ideals and ideas called anthroposophy. They believe that humans and the planet should work in unison, in harmony with one another. In the UK then, organic beauty products were on the fringe, for the hairy-leg set only. I was, and still am, quite a natural beauty girl, and have always preferred a holistic approach for myself and brought that passion into building this brand. With care and commitment – and some unexpected help from the outbreak of mad cow disease that put people off any animal-based products and boosted the plant-based vegan market – we took Dr. Hauschka from obscurity to ubiquity. Their iconic Rose Day Cream is a beauty industry hero. We worked for this brand for more than eighteen years, and we were so delighted by its success. Today, Dr. Hauschka and Weleda, a similar brand, should be and are always remembered as the true pioneers of the natural beauty care market.

Getting Started Is the Easy Part

Lots and lots of people are good at starting something – the thrill of creation – but far fewer are good at maintaining it in the long-term. The launching is the easy bit. What comes after the fun of creation is much tougher and takes staying power and perseverance. Maintaining it, growing it and surviving down-turns are the true tests of a leader. The vast majority of people can start something. Being in love with your company five, ten, twenty years from now takes mettle.

An American friend of mine, a long-time women's magazine editor, decided to create a blog with the intention of giving her writer friends a platform for their essays and articles now that all the magazines they used to write for had folded.

'I thought it'd be a part-time job,' she said. 'Just edit and post a few articles a week. No big deal. About two weeks into it, I realised how wrong I was. Editing was the least of it. Meeting with investors was a full-time job alone. I had to spend more and more time on the platform, working with tech people, hiring them, firing them, and finding better people after learning what I really needed. After a year of sixty-hour weeks and working weekends, I had to admit that my little side project had taken over my life.'

Going into her second year, she decided to expand the brand into events and conferences, but that would mean even more time. She and her husband sat down and talked about whether she was really committed to the project.

'I was. It took about two years to fully understand what I'd gotten myself into. We had to admit that more and more of our time was taken up with my blog – and it still felt very much like it was only getting started,' she said. 'I used to edit part-time, have hobbies and a relaxed home life. Now, I had a blog.'

The happy ending is that her husband decided to work part-time to support their family at home, and my friend was able to give her start-up even more. It has become a big success and is starting to make money as the brand grows and her readership expands. 'I never thought I'd start my own company, let alone at fifty-five,' she said. 'I thought I'd be slowing down now, but I'm more engaged and busier than ever.'

If you asked a hundred people if they want to own a successful business, they'd all say an emphatic, 'Yes!' But if they really understood what that takes, most of them would say, 'On second thoughts...' A senior staffer said to me once, 'At six, I want to go home to my kids and have dinner. But you're going to be here for hours still. I don't want to do what you do.' She wasn't insulting me. She was just telling me how she honestly felt, and that's all I ask for. I happen to feel differently.

The no-BS bottom line about starting your own business: if you are really determined to make it a success, dinner might have to wait.

Bigger Is Not Necessarily Better

Nowadays, you see a lot of digital start-ups launching, and then they're immediately snapped up by a larger company. Many of those founders had that very goal in mind – to get something off the ground and then cash in on it. If that's your strategy, great and congratulations. I wish you every success and I hope you do something useful and meaningful with the money. It just seems to me that if you are really passionate about something, and it's a reflection of your core values and vision, you wouldn't want to start it up to sell it off. You'd want to devote your life to it. You'll need to if you're going to work at it for five, ten or twenty years.

We have had offers and discussions around being acquired. I think of us as 'proudly independent'. What often happens when a smaller agency is swallowed up, is that the acquiring giant makes promises about creative and strategic autonomy and control. Inevitably, the smaller agency's creative team is forced to meet monthly forecasts and weekly results, and they wind up working eighteen-hour days reporting to different business units inside the gigantic corporate structure whose real goal, above all else, is driving margins and profits for shareholders. The freedom that allowed them to be creative and attractive to the acquiring giant is choked off. Within a couple of years, you have disgruntled, burned-out creatives who are fed up and hate what they do.

Twenty-five years in, my intention is to continue to grow slowly and organically. I have learned on the job that when you are larger than 200 people, employees start to become strangers. Around or just below 200, pretty much everyone knows everyone, and the atmosphere is intimate enough for people to feel they can make friendships and have good working relationships that mean something. In the world we live in now, human-to-human connectivity is very precious, and we treasure the close relationships our staffers forge. For people to really like each other, understand each other and want to work with each other they have to take the time to get to know each other. And that would go for an acquirer, too. If I could find individuals, companies or maybe the current leaders in TCS today who want to continue with the vision, improve it and dive deeper into these simple business principles, I'd always be open to any discussion. I'm fully aware that founders aren't always the best people to run companies forever and ever. They have one set of skills, but maybe not the relevant skills to take a company through a different period of its development.

START-UPS

Here are some tips on getting your business idea on paper and off the ground:

- Take that brave first step of writing down some broad-strokes ideas, even if they are complete fantasy at this point.
- Give your company an egalitarian name. Ideally, it should also reflect the product you're selling and your core ethos (think Whole Foods, Honest Harvest, The Communications Store).
- Be guided by your best intentions, your passion and a clear vision.
- Then work harder than you ever thought you possibly could.
- Have ambitious goals that go beyond the financial.
- Constantly pare down to-do lists to four or five items, and forget the rest.
- Growth and success are always about your relationships. Choose the people around you selectively.
- Getting a business off the ground is nothing compared to keeping it going and growing five, ten, twenty years down the road.

8 Crisis Management

In the world of business, there are mistakes, and then there are crises. How a company handles a crisis might be the number one predictor of a brand's success.

One company that seems to have one crisis after another is Facebook. The years 2018/19 in terms of its public relations were particularly rough for the social media giant. Facebook was found to have secretly mined the data of 50 million users with Cambridge Analytica, allowing Russians to post fake news stories that potentially influenced the 2016 US Presidential election, then CEO Mark Zuckerberg refused to appear before British Parliament to address the company's privacy breaches. Facebook hired a political opposition-research firm to attack its critics, including billionaire philanthropist George Soros who called Facebook 'a menace to society'.[1] COO Sheryl Sandberg apologized at a tech conference, saying that the company needed to 'do better'. At the time of writing, Facebook is pulling out all the stops to regain public trust. In May 2019, it banned seven controversial and inflammatory people – including Brit Milo Yiannopoulos – from the site to show that it would no longer be a safe haven for hate. How have its crises affected the company? The Federal Trade Commission is expected to fine the company $5 billion for its privacy violations, and one-quarter of its US users have deleted the app since 2018.[2]

Despite the huge fine and drop in usership, Facebook is unlikely to collapse under the weight of its multiple blunders, although the smaller associated companies did. But I do wonder, as a PR professional and crisis management expert, if the company will ever be thought of as the rebellious-yet-benevolent upstart that it was in the Oscar-winning *The Social Network* era. Its reputation has changed, and not in a good way.

Expediency, Honesty and Efficiency Are Key

When one of our brands is in crisis, our strategy is to take immediate action, be transparent about what happened, own the crisis before anyone can present an alternative explanation and then work ourselves to the bone to set things right.

The athletic footwear brand Adidas made a terrible 'tone-deaf' mistake in 2017 by sending a marketing email that read, 'Congrats, you survived the Boston Marathon!' to runners. Four years earlier, two terrorists bombed the same event, killing three and injuring hundreds. Naturally, the backlash was swift. The company immediately issued an apology that said, 'We are incredibly sorry. There was no thought given to the insensitive email subject line we sent Tuesday. We deeply apologize for our mistake.'[3] The apology came off as genuine and the company was forgiven. The next year, Adidas got another chance to market at the event and the company created personalized highlight videos for all 30,000 runners, which were gratefully received and duly posted on social media accounts.

When it was publicly revealed that the Reimann family of Germany, founders of JAB Holding Company, which controls Krispy Kreme doughnuts, Keurig coffee makers, Dr Pepper soda and Panera Bread restaurants, were Nazis who used French and Russian prisoners of war as slaves in their factories, the company chairman and managing partner Peter Harf came out to forcefully condemn it. He told the German magazine *Bild*, '[Founder] Reimann Senior and Reimann Junior were guilty. The two businessmen have passed away, but they actually belonged in prison. We were ashamed and white as sheets. There is nothing to gloss over. These crimes are disgusting.'[4] Not only did the company reveal the family history themselves (instead of trying to hide it), they announced an $11 million donation to an undisclosed charity that fights anti-Semitism. By owning their story, the company that might have been stained with Nazi ties is now associated with undoing the wrongs of the past.

The only way out of a bad situation is to jump right into it. Not too long ago, one of our beauty clients had a bona fide calamity on its hands. A potentially harmful bacterium was found in one of its products due to a factory contamination. My advice to the client was, 'Let's admit the facts, accept responsibility, tell the consumer exactly what we are doing about it and create some appropriate, relevant, authentic compensation.'

Announcing the problem frightened consumers, obviously, and we stayed up all night responding to consumer queries and making sure we were doing all we could to communicate honestly and in a timely way. We worked closely with our client on the complicated process of sorting out which product was contaminated and exactly what stores were carrying it, and quickly removing it from sale. The product was also sold online, and we were able to communicate directly with the consumers via a team of trained people at a call centre. Our client got the factory decontaminated ASAP. It was a difficult situation, and our approach was not to sweep it under the carpet, as many companies do, and to address it head-on. The client took the hit, but no one got sick and the brand recovered quickly, in part because we worked fast to fix the problem. We even got favourable editorial coverage saying how well the company had handled the consumer recall situation.

You don't get extra points for doing the right thing and handling a crisis with expediency, honesty and efficiency. It's not part of the job; it IS the job.

A Compassionate Office Makes Personal Crises Bearable

Daniel and I feel strongly about personally protecting our clients. When you reach a level of fame and success, people tend to want to knock you down. It happens all too often to some of our clients who live their lives in the public eye. Living your life in public might sound glamorous, but it comes with huge pressures and enormous drawbacks. We do an awful lot to look after those humans, not just their brand.

When a person is the face of a brand, you can't always separate the personal and the professional. Say a client or the head of a company is getting a divorce. We've been on the phone with the lawyers trying to make sure that they understand that litigating for the sake of it is going to be difficult for the children and that the tabloids are bound to try to get hold of the story. Whose benefit is that for? Is that helpful for the kids, the family, for the two people at war? Is it helpful for the brand and business? No, it is not. We try to protect our clients from useless media gossip which many people enjoy but I loathe because I've seen the damage it can do. Using other people's private problems as entertainment is total BS, isn't it? Imagine if it was you.

Perhaps I'm so sensitive to this crisis for my clients because I went through a divorce myself. 'Carry on' is the operative phrase for starting and running a business, and you need to know that going in. The demands on your time and attention are tremendous. I haven't taken many 'I really do switch off' holidays since 1995. The majority of my time is taken up by the business, still. After I had my first daughter Valentina in 1997, I returned to work three weeks later. After Darcy in 1999, I took three months away from the office but worked from home. If I didn't have the most brilliant, wonderful nanny, I never would have survived.

At that crucial and stressful time in my life as a young mother starting a business, my marriage fell apart. We were totally ill-suited, too young to marry and should never have got together. I decided to get divorced. It was, and still is, the hardest decision, but without a shadow of a doubt, the right one for us all. What got me through that personal nightmare was having a harmonious, supportive and kind workplace to go to every day, and the best business partner in the universe in Tom.

Since I worked at a compassionate office, I had the support to get me through that divorce. Later on, Tom pretty much found me my now husband, Mungo Tennant. In a way, that relationship actually began at TCS when a very handsome man walked into the office for a meeting to discuss spa and hotel development. Mungo became my husband in 2004. My business has given me so much.

Crises Can Be Turned Into Opportunities

In 2017, due to overbooking a flight bound from Chicago to Louisville, United Airlines asked a passenger to give up his seat for crew members from the airline. The passenger refused, saying he was a doctor with patients to see the next day. Security officers were called in to forcibly remove him. In the process, they gave him concussion and knocked out two of his teeth before dragging him, bloodied, down the central aisle of the plane. Other passengers took videos of the incident and posted them on social media. Despite evidence to the contrary, United initially claimed the passenger was 'disruptive and belligerent'.[5] The 'blame the victim' strategy resulted in customer scorn, cancelled reservations and a 4 per cent drop in share price. United quickly changed its response to 'heartfelt' apologizing, and vowing to make policy and training changes, which it did. The company learned from its mistakes, and customer confidence was restored.

Compare that overlong but adequate reputation rehab to a couple of fashion retailers that made horrible errors related to race.

In 2018, Swedish retailer H&M posted a photo on its website of an African American boy wearing a sweatshirt that read 'Coolest Monkey in the Jungle'. Widespread outrage on social media ensued including this tweet from Labour MP Kate Osamor: 'I was totally shocked, dismayed to say the very least, to find this online image. How do you think this imagery is an appropriate representation of a young black boy?'[6] The retailer removed the image from the website and issued a standard apology. Crisis managed, but perhaps the company's apology wasn't as sincere as it could have been.

In 2018, to promote its upcoming fashion show in Shanghai, luxury fashion brand Dolce & Gabbana posted a video on Instagram showing a childlike Chinese woman trying to eat Italian foods – spaghetti, pizza, a cannoli – with chopsticks. The imagery and voiceover were criticized for mocking Chinese culture and perpetuating stereotypes. The video was taken down, and the company issued a standard apology, but the situation was worsened when Stefano Gabbana's Instagram private messages describing Chinese people as 'ignorant dirty smelling mafia' were leaked.[7] Celebrities in China said they were boycotting the fashion show, and it was eventually cancelled.

So often companies are still so clueless about racial overtones. Granted, some things slip through the cracks, not that they should. Any ethical company that truly cares about cultural sensitivity should hire a cultural sensitivity consultant. Take a cue from Starbucks, the coffee chain, which faced a racial crisis of its own in the spring of 2018. A Philadelphia Starbucks manager called the police about two African American men who were seated at a table waiting for another person to join them and had them arrested. The incident was filmed and posted on social media, setting off a fire storm about the dangers of 'sitting while black'. The coffee company reacted, apologized and announced that it was closing all 8000 stores for a day to train employees on culture sensitivity and bias training. Some critics called it a publicity stunt, but the company provided what their employees needed – four hours of training to see how their own unconscious bias affected their customer service. Starbucks lost millions in sales during that day, proving a commitment to improve.[8] Now it is seen as an agent of change where all are welcomed to sit or use the toilet, no purchase required.

Every problem can be transitioned into a solution. Every crisis can be an opportunity for a company to define itself as one that responds with compassion and responsibility, or one that doesn't. Without a doubt, bosses and companies should aspire to avoid crises, but they will arise, and how they are then dealt with is just as crucial to the future of a company or brand as what actually happened.

Stay the Course Against Unethical Enemies

TCS's first 'office' was a desk in a windowless workspace my then-husband rented. I shared it with two men – an American called Bob and a friend called Ali, who made me laugh and kept my confidence up, even when I had some dark days in the beginning. Bob was a techie, an early adopter of the World Wide Web, and he told me that TCS should have a website. 'It's the future of communications,' he said. Boy, was he right about that. Bob very generously built a basic site for me with a home page, information about clients and contact info.

This rudimentary website nearly destroyed my new company. It brought about a crisis I could never have anticipated. No matter how expert your business plan and financial projections, something is bound to come up that you can't prepare for. Just when you think you've covered every possible base, something might pop up out of nowhere and take you down.

In my case, it was a lawsuit. Shortly after my website went live, I was sued by a former employer. These were the nascent days of HTML. No one knew how it worked or what it would become. What happened was that I had put my CV on my little website. The only presence of my former employer's company on the Internet was on my site, on that CV. (No one had websites at the time; if it weren't for Bob, I wouldn't have had one either.) A legal letter arrived and accused me of inverse passing off. In basic terms, I was accused of using another company's establishment and reputation to promote my own new business.

I hadn't misrepresented myself or done anything wrong. Nonetheless, the legal bills were coming in and crushing me right out of the gate. This lawsuit was groundbreaking, actually – there was no precedent yet about anything web-related – and it was covered in the British press by my university friend Vicky Ward, now a hugely successful author, broadcaster and journalist for *Vanity Fair*, then a junior reporter at the *Independent*.

As I recall, her headline screamed, 'PR Fur Flies on the World Wide Web!' I'd prayed night after night for some publicity to announce my new company, but not like this.

The lawyers were relentless. At 5 p.m. every Friday for a year, I'd get a call or a fax from them with queries that would really shake me up; things like, 'Cambridge University doesn't seem to have any record of Julietta Dexter being a student at Jesus College, Cambridge, between 1988 and 1991. Please provide certified evidence of this alleged fact.' Every aspect of my life and my CV was pulled apart. I wasted weeks proving that what I'd written was true and that I was an upstanding citizen who hadn't lied or cheated to get ahead. Meanwhile, I was pregnant, and struggling physically, certainly emotionally and definitely financially.

One day, I went to *Vogue* for a hugely sought-after meeting and was so overwhelmed, I burst into tears. Editor Clarissa Brooke-Turner was beyond kind and asked me what was going on. I apologized profusely for crying in her office and blurted out the story. 'I don't think I can manage it,' I said. At that point I knew that I could not afford the legal fees. I was seven months pregnant with my first child. Running the few accounts we had won frankly became the easiest part of my life. All my ideals, my values, my enthusiasm for 'starting a business' were being blown away. At times, over my career, I've woken in the night in a cold sweat, terror running through my body. This was one of those times. The fear was all-consuming, not just of failure (that's good for you) but of going under, having huge legal fees to pay and not being able to provide for my child. It was more than I could handle. My husband was not able to support me in any way, and our marriage was another huge source of stress.

Clarissa knew the industry, knew the players and, frankly, she'd been generous to take a meeting with a start-up newbie like me. Without so much as a second thought, she groaned, rolled her eyes heavenwards and said, 'Oh, don't worry, this is a pattern. When young competitors come into the market, the best thing to do is to try and destroy them. I think you're being bullied. Stay strong.'

Clarissa's words were a huge comfort. I'd never thought of it like that. Soon after, I met another previous employer who confirmed pretty much the same thing.

One thing I am able to do is admit when I have done something wrong. I don't hesitate to apologize. If I'd made a mistake in this case, I would have closed up shop and probably berated myself for the rest of my life. But I knew that I had done nothing wrong, and certainly not something illegal. I had moments of nearly losing my mind, thinking that if the lawyers really believed I'd committed a crime, then I must have. I was just too young, ignorant and naïve to understand the law.

After months of endless legal communication, my baby was cooking and my lawyer suggested bringing the court date forward so I wouldn't give birth on the defendant's table (my due date and court date nearly coincided exactly). I was playing with fire, but I also knew that between fighting a lawsuit and having a baby, the latter was going to be more important, whatever the outcome of the former.

My lawyer communicated with the other side, and then called me with shocking news. They had decided to 'drop' the suit! Just like that. It was a case with no precedent. In the end, the other side had to cover all my legal bills. My lawyer at the time felt we should have counter-sued for harassment, but I just wanted to get on with my life. I went through an enormous amount of pain over what was, it seemed to me, a tactic to frighten, scare and undermine me. No wonder I feel so passionately about being fair, decent and honest!

Ironically, Bob the Techie told me that only fourteen people had ever even looked at my website, and ten were my friends and family. A storm in a teacup almost broke me. Having a little cry or, actually, being human in front of Clarissa – what you're not supposed to do – is what gave me the comfort and strength to carry on.

Be Realistic

One of the wisest pieces of advice in business is to be a generally positive, thankful person. Positivity should not be equated with optimism. Many professions (especially mine) are populated by good news people who want to tell you that everything is fabulous and fun and fantastic all the time. But often that's simply not the case, and being too overconfident opens the door to unacceptable ineptitude and poor preparation. That is not real life.

I take my cues about positivity from one of the most astonishing human beings I've been privileged to meet, Mark Pollock. At the age of five, Mark lost the sight in his right eye. That didn't stop him from becoming a competitive rower at Trinity

College in Dublin where he studied business and economics. At the age of twenty-two, in 1998, he also lost the sight in his left eye. Total blindness didn't stop him, either, and he went on to win bronze and silver medals in the Commonwealth Rowing Championships in 2002, run six marathons, hike across the Gobi Desert to raise thousands for charity, finish the North Pole marathon in 2004, and, in a truly astonishing feat, trek 779 kilometres, pulling a 90-kilogram sled, to the South Pole as part of a three-man team, coming fifth in the 2009 Amundsen Omega 3 Race. These would be huge accomplishments for anyone, let alone a man who has lost his sight.

A year and a half after the South Pole expedition, a few weeks before his wedding, Mark fell out of a second-storey window, suffered a traumatic spinal injury and was paralyzed from the waist down. As an athlete, this blow could have devastated him, but even this tragedy didn't stop Mark from living his best life and being an inspiration to all those who are lucky enough to cross his path.

I invited Mark to be the key speaker at our company away day a few years ago. He gave the most remarkable speech about the difference between pessimism, realism and optimism. He believes that people who do well aren't optimistic. They don't hope for the best. They're realistic and deal with the facts at hand. Whether he was pulling a sled to the South Pole or lying in a hospital bed waiting to find out if he would ever walk again, he had to be realistic about his situation. If he pumped himself up every day, saying, 'Yeah, this is fine, this is so cool, everything's going to be great,' he would have been deceiving himself and setting himself up for potentially crushing disappointment that could have brought on severe depression. If he went to the other extreme and said, 'This is the worst-case scenario,' his negative energy would have made sure he'd remain down in the dumps. Instead, he took things minute by minute, hour by hour, appreciated what he had, and chose not to look at the point of arrival, but to see the scope of his journey and all its potential destinations.

Mark is a realist who strives for the best-case scenario. He's working with new science and technology companies with the goal of becoming the first paralyzed person to walk again, along with keeping up with his writing career and travelling the world as a motivational speaker on the subjects of innovation, collaboration and resilience. Not only is he busier and more accomplished than most able-bodied people, he is so self-aware and open to whatever life has in store for him.

I very much try to follow Mark's philosophy of realism, which he articulates and embodies perfectly. Pessimism only goes down one route – a negative one. But optimism comes with its own dangers. If you're too hopeful, you might not act with due diligence, care, attention, preparation or humility. I consider myself a realist, and I serve my staff and clients by ensuring that I take things at face value, step by step, and this helps us move forward together on a journey.

It's important to aim for an outcome but not to predetermine it. Be ready and flexible for bumps that may appear in the road. I am a real planner; my brain works by setting goals and strategies, and I find it difficult when things aren't achieved by a certain date or as I plan them. You could argue that this is a strength, but what if, like Mark, life takes its own course?

Your ability to be flexible, to adapt, to accept that you can't just determine an outcome is key to your success and your happiness.

Don't Get Too Comfortable

A common mistake people make is to assume that things are going well and they have no cause for concern. Not so! As a boss or team leader, one has to keep a close eye on every element of the business at all times. As soon as a boss thinks, 'I've worked really hard to get to this place, so now I can relax', that's when things are sure to go wrong. Right under one's nose, a crisis might be brewing.

In 2018, our company sustained a financial crisis that we did not see coming. We've had great times since then, and it is wonderful to talk about that crisis as something that is now well in the past. In short, we made a very, very bad decision and failed to keep a close watch on certain areas of the business. I can't provide specific details, for legal reasons, but suffice it to say that by the time we'd figured out what was going on, we were in trouble. After shepherding TCS through twenty-four years of steady growth (with a couple of downturns, I admit), I was completely blindsided by this attack out of nowhere.

I ignored some red flags and, for that, I'll never stop blaming myself. Granted, we were very busy and focused on a strong strategic plan for evolving our business by building a brilliant VIP and Events team, and a growing Creative, Innovation, Insight and Digital team. We'd also decided to plant a flag much more publicly in a fundamentally important part of consumerism – conscious consumerism, which means paying attention to the environmental and social impact of products, and brands that don't align with your ideals – and we brought in an expert to head up the area of Purpose, Responsibility and Sustainability. We'd decided to make our business global and open an office in New York. With so much going on and the company growing in an intelligent, innovative and integrated way, and with so many exciting accounts coming in, my attention was diverted from the basics – the incoming and outgoing, the contacts, logistics – and that was where things went wrong. Being busy elsewhere is no excuse. As the boss, it was my job to know exactly what was going on, and not to let 'everyday' things slide. In hindsight, I ignored my instincts and I was not exacting enough. Once the crisis was fully revealed, it took us six months of nineteen-hour workdays to dig our way out of a very deep hole. I came to a big realisation: a company can be destroyed in just a few weeks but saving it can take months, if not years.

Thanks to the understanding and dedication of our leaders, our chairman, our management team, our employees and our clients – and the endless, patient support of my husband – we got through it. Our bank was solid, decent and willing to work with us and help us out. I guess they'd seen things like this before. The most important lesson I learned during that nightmare year is that in all businesses and in all walks of life, you trust others or you don't. If you do, like me, sometimes, thankfully rarely, your trust can be massively abused with really desperate consequences. That is reality.

When you are pushed to the brink, you learn exactly what you're made of. I worked harder than ever, even harder maybe than when I founded the company. I thought I knew my limits – from the sheer number of hours and days I could go without a break, to how quickly I can learn new skills – but I pushed past them and forced myself to destroy the restrictive self-beliefs of 'I'm not very good at that, so I won't do it.' I had no other choice but to do so. This crisis, for all its misery, gave me deeper insight into what I'm capable of. In early middle age, I learned that I am capable of more than I thought possible. I found another two gears in me that I never knew I had.

We are *all* capable of so much more than we think. We are all one crisis away from realizing our full potential. It's a bit like your body – go hard in the gym, and your body does much more than you thought it could. The mind is the same. Mistakes are an opportunity to discover. Hard times are a chance to grow, and to appreciate everything you have. Once you learn you can move mountains in a crisis, you realize you can do it anytime if you work your passion, wisdom, strength and attention to detail with relentless rigour.

I was not alone. Four extraordinary people were around me. And even if I do say so myself, we were actually unbelievable. We did not waste a second playing the blame game. One way or another, we instantly accepted and agreed that we'd all been a bit too trusting, maybe a little too relaxed. We didn't miss a heartbeat spending time wondering 'what if?' or 'if only' or 'if you had done that...' We just put our arms around each other, as a team, and fixed it.

WALK THE WALK

To the managers and supervisors reading this book, and for those dreaming of starting their own company one day, be the leader you wished you'd had when you were just starting out. Be the honourable role model who people take their cues from. Don't just talk it when you are giving your keynote but act it out in practice each and every day. Inspire people to be their best selves and do their finest work – by being your best self and doing your best work. Leadership is a privilege and a responsibility to serve and protect the people who work so hard for your department or company's success. Role-modelling ethical values and behaviours is a duty of care to others.

I have defined success in part as doing all that I can to provide for our people and make them great, trying to help them fulfil themselves. When I shared with the staff and clients that we were not in a great place and would be hand-to-mouth for quite a while, every one of the people I'd been working so hard to care for stepped up to take care of me.

It was remarkable, extraordinary and humbling. I will never forget the kindnesses granted to us when we needed them most. Even the incredible people we had no other choice but to make redundant were so heartbreakingly understanding about it. I cried hard about them (but not in front of them). Without question, our relationships and our values saved us. Since they were based on trust and genuine care, these connections stayed strong, our passion never waned and we used every ounce of our collective wisdom – and our hard work ethic – to find solutions. Throughout this period, we cheered each other on, and consoled each other through some very dark moments.

Being in the thick of a crisis reveals the depth of one's ethics, honesty and compassion. If we'd failed to live up to our values, we wouldn't have come out the other side. There is always a temptation to lie one's way out of trouble or to turn on others to protect oneself. But if a person in crisis can stay strong, wise and caring, they'll not only survive, but will be that much stronger, wiser and caring the next time the wheel of fortune turns.

For ethical leaders, crises are only an opportunity to serve as examples of how to keep up one's hope, faith and morals. It's so easy to be inspirational when things are going great, but when the chips are down, your finest qualities are revealed.

The key is also to act and act fast. Don't spend any time at all hoping it might not be so bad and pretending that nothing is wrong. Be honest.

CRISIS MANAGEMENT

No one likes being in turmoil, but bad times will happen and how you handle them could be the end or a new beginning for your career or company.

- The crisis might not be your fault, but if you don't take immediate steps to fix it, it won't matter what or who caused the trouble in the first place.

- Never hide a problem. As they say in politics, 'The cover up is worse than the crime.' Get in front of a crisis by admitting to it.
- Even if someone is using unethical tactics against you, return fire with compassion, kindness and truth. You might lose the battle, but you'll keep your integrity and reputation as an ethical person.
- A cruel act can be countered with a kind one. But words aren't enough. Take action to correct poor judgement.
- Rely on the compassionate people around you to help you get through rough times.
- Use your strength and wisdom to inspire others to keep going until the crisis is over.
- A crisis is a mirror that shows you what you're really made of. Don't look away.

9 Responsibility

In 2015, Volkswagen received the top rating for automakers on the Dow Jones Sustainability Index and the company put out a statement bragging about their commitment to climate-friendliness. *One week later*, the US Environmental Protection Agency's investigation concluded that Volkswagen had been using illegal devices that rigged their car's software to make their emissions levels look safer than they actually were. For six years, certain executives had put out fraudulent data.

Ironically, Volkswagen's official code of conduct includes statements such as, 'We stand for responsible, honest actions' and 'We are obligated to the truth with respect to political institutions.'[1] Why would a company as well-respected as Volkswagen spend money to design and install software made to hide the truth? Easy: it thought it was cheaper to lie than to build a better engine that might cost some money.

The carmaker immediately felt the impact of the scandal. It was removed from the Dow Jones Sustainability Index, lost 40 per cent of its share price and all its credibility, and, at the time of writing, its global fines and losses due to this scandal – 'the bill' – are over $25 billion.[2] CEO Martin Winterkorn has been charged with fraud by German and American prosecutors. Not only did Volkswagen put profit over people, it put profit over the planet. That more or less sums up a company's failure to act responsibly in pursuit of short-term gain and growth at all costs. Can we now no longer trust the veracity of sustainability indexes either?

Scaling up is a hot topic for most business owners, since it's widely believed that unless you are growing in size, you are slowly dying. A responsible company might do well to worry less about scaling up and, instead, strive consciously to scale *out* to make a mission of doing honest, good work for the benefit of its people, the consumers of its products, and the places and people impacted by its business.

At TCS, we have a senior leader dedicated to this now – an expert in sustainability, purpose, responsibility and conscious consumerism. Her entire job is to help us work hard to become more and more of a 'conscious' company and help us work with our clients and make sure that they are what they say they are, and that they uphold real values of purpose, responsibility and sustainability. The truth is that all of us – all brands, all humans in the developed world – need to focus on this. One way or another, the explosion of consumerism over the last thirty years or so has taken its toll on the planet and its inhabitants. We are still in a place where brands are nervous about putting their hand in the air, terrified that an investigative journalist will go undercover and find that factory with poor social conditions that they did not even know was part of their supply chain because it is so big. The 's' word of sustainability may not quite yet be perceived as super sexy, but a movement is starting all around us. It is exciting, very. It's true – reading a sustainability report is not like reading *Vanity Fair*. While some brands are doing a great job at putting sustainability front and centre, other more established brands are worried that it might cost them too much money to change to a more sustainable supply chain. At TCS, we are working with clients in a really open way. We are not finger-pointing but realizing that we have all got it wrong and working out how we can all work together to improve. No judgement, just improvement.

Only Work with People Who Care

We take great care in choosing the people and brands we work with at TCS. Every client and company is really carefully considered before we represent them. We do searches for lawsuits, scandals and evidence against them on social or environmental issues. It's a super complex subject, and our senior director of responsibility, sustainability and purpose, Esther Maughan McLachlan, has taught the leadership team so much about how to look in to all companies efficiently. We look into the conditions in their factories and research any human rights violations and company history. If we find any problems, we say, 'Listen, we're really sorry but we don't feel that we can work with you because of x, y and z.'

Several times, clients have said, 'Okay, what would we have to do to work together?' Companies are beginning to change and some even improve their supply chains and switch to sustainable products in order to make change and make it fast. It sounds so arrogant to say, but I do believe that because we are known to turn down business on ethical grounds, our working with a client is, in and of itself, a stamp of approval. This would not be the case if we didn't uphold ethics and honesty as our core values.

The opposite side of this would be a company that willingly worked with unsavoury clients, and risked being brought down by their association. Business page readers will be familiar with the saga of PR agency Bell Pottinger's involvement in a South African election, setting off an international firestorm over their use of incendiary social media accounts that pushed blatantly false claims and fanned racial tensions. This election scandal, its ensuing cross-continental protests, the company's ejection from the Public Relations and Communications Association in the UK and a take-no-prisoners, in-house battle between founder Tim Bell and CEO James Henderson brought down the thirty-year-old agency and put all the people who worked there out of a job.[3] There is no question in my mind that the staff at Bell Pottinger were decent people. Lives were destroyed, a nation's political process damaged and what was it all for? Short-term profit and influence? Not a sustainable, or responsible, business model.

Invest in Being Conscious

Caring is fundamentally about the values of a business: how one treats people and the planet. One of the brands I admire in this regard is Patagonia, the outdoor clothing brand. Its founder, inventor and adventurer, Yvon Chouinard, has written about how his love of the outdoors led him to become, as he called himself, 'a reluctant businessman'[4] who was motivated by exploring nature, not raking in the millions.* His business philosophy is: greed is wrong, invest in your own people, give back a percentage of your profits to environmental causes and don't waste resources. The company is quite literally chang- ing the world with how much it cares about its customers and the places they go. Since 1985, the company has donated $89 million to environmental causes. Through their venture capital- ist fund Tin Shed Ventures, Patagonia has donated an additional $75 million to socially and environmentally minded compa- nies that are repurposing plastic waste, detoxifying water and installing solar panels. Chouinard's charity, 1% for the Planet, has donated $175 million to environmental groups since 2002. In 2019, CEO Rose Marcario announced that the company was donating their tax windfall (President Trump cut corporate tax rates in 2017) to climate change charities. 'Being a responsible company means paying your taxes in proportion to your success and supporting your state and federal governments, which in turn contribute to the health and well-being of civil society,' she said. 'We are giving away this tax cut to the planet, our only home, which needs it now more than ever.'[5]

Lyft, the American ride-hailing company, has proven to its customers that it cares about the world we live in, and all of its

---

* Writer/photographer Jeff Johnson retraced Chouinard's epic 1968 explorations in Patagonia and made it an inspiring 2010 movie called *180° South*, which I highly recommend.

people. In 2018, the company announced a plan to neutralize the environment impact of its 1.4 million cars on the road by buying millions of dollars' worth of 'carbon offsets', or investments in projects aimed at reducing carbon emissions. The company's president and co-founder John Zimmer described it as 'a tax on ourselves'.[6] What's more, Lyft makes it easy for its customers to contribute to the charities of their choice with Round Up & Donate. Via the app, customers can donate the 'round up' change of the nearest dollar to human rights organizations, children's hospitals and arts charities.

Not only does this move demonstrate care, it's good business. A company that goes out of its way to be responsible is appealing to consumers. According to a 2015 study of some 9700 consumers from nine countries, 91 per cent of consumers around the world want companies to be responsible for social and environmental issues, 84 per cent would actively look for responsible products and 90 per cent would boycott a known-to-be-irresponsible or unethical company.[7]

Compare Lyft's culture of responsibility to its main competitor in the ride-hailing space – Uber, a company that, in 2017, lost its licence in London because of its irresponsible practices with background checks of drivers and failure to report crimes to the police. (In 2018, they got a probationary licence to operate in London for a fifteen-month review period.)[8] Uber had serious problems in its corporate offices as well. Its founder Travis Kalanick left the company after staffers went public with complaints about gender discrimination and sexual harassment; a year later, in 2018, Uber agreed to pay $1.9 million to fifty-six women who'd been victimized at the company.[9] That settlement came shortly after a top executive at the company was forced to resign under investigation for racial discrimination.[10]

Since all of Uber's scandals began in 2017, Lyft has been gaining ground on its once-dominant competitor. As of mid-2018, Lyft claimed to hold 35 per cent of the market compared to 20 per cent in 2017.[11] Uber's reputation might have something do to with why its initial public offering (IPO) on the New York Stock Exchange was considered to be a massive disappointment or, as described in *The New York Times*, a 'train wreck'.[12]

Care about the Community

As co-founder Sergey Brin once famously said to the architects who designed Google's San Francisco campus, 'No one should be more than 200 feet away from food.'[13] Staffers also have on-site access to haircuts, laundry service, nap areas and day care. Just about any human need is a short walk from your desk. San Francisco-based Twitter and Menlo Park-based Facebook are also famous for their all-you-can-eat gourmet sushi bars and the ever-present, non-stop flow of meals for its people.

These services are great for Facebook, Twitter and Google staffers. However, they are not so good for the local communities. If no one ever leaves the tech giants' campuses, the streets around them are deserted. With no foot traffic, the local shops and restaurants are starved of customers and, not surprisingly, go out of business.

In 2018, the San Francisco legislature put forth a proposal that all new office constructions in the city limits would be banned from having an on-site cafeteria to force workers to hit the streets and spread some of their hefty Silicon Valley salaries around the community. Similar legislation was initiated in Mountain View, California, the location for a new Facebook office building. I agree with the zoning initiatives. It's not enough for a company to feed its people, it has to feed the community, too. There's also something contradictory for me here, in Google's motives. Are they saying, 'We love our staff, we want them to work hard, but we don't want them to leave the building'? The well-being of our staff means that they should take a walk outside, they should go home, they should rest.

Some companies are so committed to improving their communities that they give employees incentives to do so. TCC is an American wireless retail company, one of many in a crowded field. To differentiate itself and make it more attractive to the Millennials that make up 85 per cent of its workforce, TCC launched a programme called Culture of Good. After carrying out market research and finding out that its workforce embraced the 'buy local' ideal, TCC focused its charitable programmes on local communities. As participants in Culture of Good, employees get sixteen hours of paid time off per year to volunteer in their own neighbourhoods. In 2015, TCC was able to donate $1.2 million to local schools, backpack giveaways, tree planting and tinned food drives, with much gratitude and appreciation all around. And in return, TCC enjoys an 11 per cent higher employee retention rate than its competitors.[14] Since its people are highly visible in schools, parks and community centres, it's like free advertising that brings in more customers.

Give Back to the People Who Do the Work

A company might put all-natural on the label, but it can really prove its ethical standards by passing on its brand mandate to the people who create the products. Caring begins at home, with employees.

In the UK, skincare company Dr. Hauschka had its offices on a big plot on what was once farmland. It converted some of the acreage into a biodynamic vegetable farm in keeping with the company's all-natural principles. Every Monday, an email was sent out to staff listing the harvest of crops for that week, and the employees wrote back to place their order for however many tomatoes or cucumbers they'd like to take home that Thursday. Providing a box of organic vegetables for each employee is a clear demonstration of how seriously Dr. Hauschka cares about, and for, the health and wellness of its people and the planet.

Harmless Harvest, an organic coconut water brand, has the word 'harmless' in its name. It advertises being an 'ecosystem-based business' that supports the welfare of its farmers in rural Thailand, invests in their communities, harvests coconuts sustainably and touts its fair trade certification. Calling attention to the flavour of the water itself is almost an afterthought. (It's delicious, by the way.)

Raise Standards

The trend towards ethical practices in one business raises standards for entire industries. When one company sees the great press another gets for supporting its workers and community, the competitor has to follow suit or look bad in comparison. The positive impact extends to consumers as well. They gravitate towards companies that are doing right by their communities and avoid those that aren't. Individuals want to make the world a better place, but they're not always in a position to do as much good as a company can. So, if you know that Whole Foods donates produce to homeless shelters and food banks (which it does), you'll feel noble about shopping there and will pay a little more for that positive vibe.

A stunning example of a brand changing its practices to keep up with ethical standards is Perdue, one of America's largest chicken farms. They saw their customers, especially the under-thirty-five-year-olds, fleeing to organic, cage-free, cruelty-free farms in droves. In response, Perdue partnered with the Humane Society to completely overhaul its massive breeding operations. Antibiotics, indoor barns and inhumane slaughtering methods were out. Natural light, airy outdoor space and humane treatment of the animals on their one very bad day were initiated. The chairman of the company, Jim Perdue, has said that the many millions it cost the company to make these changes will pay off in the end with increased sales.[15] He gets it. You have to give the customer what they want, and his customers want healthy, happy birds. But in the meantime, as the standard-bearer, Perdue is setting a new high bar for competitors.

Use Good Judgement

Being responsible isn't always so clear-cut. Despite believing in animal rights, I have worn fur. It's a much more complicated choice than one might think. In northern Italy, where I grew up, wearing fur is, generally speaking, not considered offensive. However, fur's acceptability in certain parts of the world is not a justification for the poor treatment of animals.

From a sustainability standpoint, I think about it a great deal, and whether or not our company should represent furriers. The reality is, the global demand for fur is not going away. According to the London-based International Fur Federation statistics, the fur trade is a $3.7-billion business, with over 70 million mink pelts harvested annually.[16] Fake fur is not an ideal solution because it's made with non-biodegradable petroleum. So, after having considered every angle, we made the choice to be a proponent of humane, sustainable farming and represent Saga Furs, a company that is a strong advocate for the environment and known for its humane treatment of animals. It is not so much about saying whether wearing fur is right or wrong, but rather if you are going to do so, do it in the most humane, sustainable and responsible way you can. In the end, however, I still struggle with this issue.

You do the best you can, and then try to exceed those efforts. It can start small, but if every employee, team and department checked in with how the office operated in a planet-friendly way, collectively we could make a bit of a difference. Perhaps you campaign for wooden coffee stirrers instead of plastic ones or convert customers to paper-free billing. Even having fair trade standards for cafeteria snacks is a step in the right direction.

Work Together to Give Back

A perfect example of what I've been saying all along about the good business of ethics, kindness and generosity came from inside TCS. Jo Jones has worked in beauty her whole adult life. She knows the business inside out and has a real appreciation for the power of grooming. Giving someone access to basic hygiene products that they'd otherwise not have can really change their outlook and raise their dignity. So she and Sali Hughes (one of the UK's most valued beauty writers) had the brilliant idea of stockpiling products for the homeless who don't have the money to buy the things we all take for granted, such as deodorant, shampoo, body wash, razors, shaving gel, towels, tampons, toilet paper, toothbrushes and hairbrushes, and to organize a distribution system to get the products into the hands of those who need them.

They called the initiative Beauty Banks.

'Can I do it from our TCS offices and store supplies here?' Jo asked me.

I loved the idea and said, 'Go for it.'

Jo was very excited about this way to give back, but she couldn't do it without the products themselves. So, at the beginning, she went to talk to some of the big beauty companies to ask for their help. They basically ignored her, but she and Sali didn't give up and their persistence paid off. Jo and

Sali were able to get some good press to promote the idea and created social media accounts for it. They set up a wish list of products on Amazon for people to send to our address in Kensington Square. I walked into the office one day, and the entire place was piled high with cardboard boxes full of donations. The next step was to partner up and use the national infrastructure of food banks to distribute these products, which has gone beautifully.

Jo was doing all this on top of her full-time job, and that was a lot to take on. As a company, we asked Esther, our senior director of responsibility, sustainability and purpose, to help, share strategies from similar initiatives she'd seen, and pitch in whatever ideas she had. We asked any available staffers to help get the products into sorted boxes. Our office remained the shipping depot and warehouse for a while, until a logistics company came forward and offered to help. Everyone pitched in in some way. And now that it's up and running and so successful, the big beauty companies that may have ignored Jo and Sali the first time around are now very keen to get on board.

Soon after, Beauty Banks came up in a new business pitch. We were preparing for a big pitch to a company we would love to work with. The Body Shop is a classic British brand that was founded by an incredible, pioneering activist: the late, great Anita Roddick. She died far too young, but her spirit remains. An environmental activist and true 'green' pioneer, she was talking about fair trade and organic natural products back in the 1970s. The Body Shop was shopping for a new communications company to work on brand development, and we were invited to a pitch parade with four or five other agencies.

We went in for our meeting and did our prepared pitch to some senior executives. Their eyes were glazed over, with lots of nodding and 'Okay, yep. Go on.' It didn't feel like our words were landing. Finally, one exec said, 'Tell me something interesting and really meaningful about TCS.'

I said, 'Well, I honestly think you'd be more interested in this initiative that has been headed up by Jo Jones, our senior beauty director.'

The guy from The Body Shop had been sitting back in his chair, his arms crossed in front of his chest. When he heard about the Beauty Banks, he leaned forward and started listening. We got into the nitty-gritty about how Jo and Sali had founded Beauty Banks, and how it's evolved into a lobbying effort to get the sales tax removed from tampons and a push to supply every homeless person in the UK with a sanitary kit of toiletries.

Before we started talking about Beauty Banks, he hadn't been so interested in us. But the bit that caught his attention and spoke to this very senior level beauty executive was Jo's initiative. I can absolutely guarantee that the very last reason Jo and Sali started Beauty Banks was to impress any client, ever. They started Beauty Banks because they work in a brilliant industry and they wanted to do some good with the network and contacts they had.

I absolutely love the direction the world is turning towards; that a company that uses its skills and resources to help people attracts other business that shares the same charitable, honest and decent spirit. It's just phenomenal. It feels like a real sea change. People are really getting it – that it's not enough just to make money. You have to change people's lives for the better and build connections and relationships that stretch from one desk to the next, and all the way around the globe.

RESPONSIBILITY

It might be too reductive to say all corporate responsibility could be summed up with the phrase 'do unto others' but as a guiding ideal, it works. The finer points:

- Instead of just focusing on scaling up, ethical companies should scale out, taking the mission of doing good beyond the business and into the industry and beyond.
- Corporate responsibility begins with whom you work with. Hire, collaborate and partner with ethical people.
- It's not enough to do well by your employees, you also have to support your company's community.
- Consumers will spend more money on a product if they know the company is protecting the environment and doing good works.

Conclusion
Success

The founder of The Body Shop, Anita Roddick, once said, 'There's no scientific answer for success. You can't define it. You've simply got to live it and do it.'[1]

Every person has his or her own idea of what 'being successful' means. For some, it means making more money than they could ever spend in multiple lifetimes, aka 'winning' on a grand scale. Others might view it as reaching the top of their field and clinging to that perch for dear life, no matter what. For some, it might mean starting a company, writing a book or creating a product that makes a positive impact on the world.

When I was younger, I was driven by achievement and followed the traditional path towards success. I went to school and university, did my best and then went out to earn a living. Once I'd joined the workforce, I didn't always like what I saw and rebelled against other people's methods of getting to 'successful'. I resolved to make our company a success on our own ethical, compassionate terms.

As I got older and hopefully a teeny bit wiser, I stopped thinking about success as something I needed to care about. I could do better asking myself how well I was serving others, maybe setting an example and being a useful guide. My father is my role model in business because he didn't bother with the BS concept of success based on ego and money, and instead focused on how kindly and fairly he treated everyone. I just try to live by a set of moral codes such as, 'Do unto others' and weigh my so-called achievement on that.

Of course, it's tempting to find some simple metric, like net worth or the size of one's office. But people who measure their success in pounds and titles are never satisfied. Every time they hit a new benchmark, they just double it. Striving for 'success' in one aspect of life might result in failure in another. It might cause harm to people close by, and those far away. Amassing money alone means nothing, but if one used financial resources responsibly with a positive purpose for the planet and its people, that would be a success.

Objectively, others might define TCS as a success because we're still thriving after twenty-five years, have launched and grown hundreds of brands, and supported the lives of so many wonderful, talented, hard-working people. But I don't use the s-word to define my company. I prefer to use words like 'purposeful', 'sustainable' and 'responsible'. As for myself, I go with 'grateful' and 'fortunate'. Every day, I think about how blessed I've been to be able to come to work and do what I do with such amazing people around me. My health and family have supported me in being able to keep doing it. When I've had a bad day at work, when things go wrong and I feel overwhelmed, I remind myself how fortunate I've been and how grateful I am.

If I've achieved anything, it's because of the work of so many others as well as my own – Tom, Daniel, my colleagues. No single person can say, 'I'm a self-made man/woman' because no one gets there alone. Humility should be the default setting of any leader because they are nothing without their team. I would never want to place myself or anyone else on that pedestal. I don't deserve it.

As people start and go forward in their careers, I hope they keep in mind the no-BS business principles I've described here – the ethos of compassion, the joy of collaboration and the relief of honesty. Ethical companies are not only more profitable, but also more pleasant to work at. The bottom line for anyone who wants to work at or lead a no-BS business is to serve clients, customers and colleagues to the best of one's ability; to treat (and pay) workers fairly and equally; to let women do their jobs without throwing obstacles in their path; to use clear, considered communications that send a positive, truthful message; to own mistakes and immediately work to fix them; to work together for the benefit of all; and to be decent humans. If we can all strive for those principles, which I'd call both optimistic and realistic, we just might be able to save ourselves and the world, one ethical, compassionate business at a time.

Endnotes

Introduction The Future Is Friendly

1   Solon, O. and Laughland, O. (2 May 2018). Cambridge Analytica closing after Facebook data harvesting scandal. *The Guardian*.

2   Butler, S. (25 Apr. 2016). How Philip Green's family made millions as value of BHS plummeted. *The Guardian*.

3   Butler, S. (4 May 2019). Philip Green tries to stop Topshop group falling like house of cards by Sarah Butler. *The Guardian*.

4   Strategy&. What happens after a legendary CEO departs? https://www.strategyand.pwc.com/ceosuccess.

5   Health and Safety Executive (31 Oct. 2018). Work related stress depression or anxiety statistics in Great Britain, 2018. http://www.hse.gov.uk/statistics/causdis/stress.pdf.

6   American Psychological Association (4 Feb. 2015). Stress in America: Paying with our health. https://www.apa.org/news/press/releases/stress/2014/stress-report.pdf.

7   Gelles, D. (28 Aug. 2018). In Elon Musk's world, brakes are for cars, not C.E.O.s. *New York Times*.

8   Georgescu, P. (26 Jul. 2017). Doing the right thing is just profitable. *Forbes*.

9   McKinsey & Company (Jan. 2018). Delivering through diversity. https://www.mckinsey.com/~/media/mckinsey/business%20

functions/organization/our%20insights/delivering%20
through%20diversity/delivering-through-diversity_full-report.
ashx.

10 Nyberg, A. (2 Nov. 2009). Poor leadership poses a health risk at work. Karolinska Institute.

11 EY (2015). Global generations: A global study on work-life challenges across generations. https://www.ey.com/Publication/ vwLUAssets/Global_generations_study/$FILE/EY-global- generations-a-global-study-on-work-life-challenges-across- generations.pdf.

12 Center for Women and Business, Bentley University (2017). Multigenerational impacts on the workplace. https://www.bentley. edu/centers/center-for-women-and-business/multigenerational- impacts-research-report-request.

1 Leadership

1 Sainato, M. (1 Dec. 2018). Laid-off Sears workers left with nothing – and they say wealthy bosses are to blame. *The Guardian*.

2 Wang, U. (25 Oct. 2013). Campbell Soup CEO: 'You can lead the change or be a victim of change'. *The Guardian*.

3 Valet, V. (17 May 2018). The world's most reputable CEOs 2018. *Forbes*.

4 Ardehali, R. (18 Apr. 2019). Sears sues billionaire former chairman Eddie Lampert and Treasury Secretary Steven Mnuchin claiming they illegally siphoned billions of dollars of assets from retailer before it went bankrupt. *Daily Mail*.

5 Tepper, B. J., Simon, L. and Park, H. M. (2017). Abusive supervision. *Annual Review of Organizational Psychology and Organizational Behavior*, 4, 123–52.

6 Newell, C., Dixon, H. and Investigations Team (8 Feb. 2019). Sir

Philip Green's accusers: The allegations told for the first time. *Daily Telegraph*.

7   Sweney, M. (8 Feb. 2019). Philip Green faces £3m legal bill as new abuse allegations published. *The Guardian*.

8   Wong, J. C. (22 Apr. 2019). Demoted and sidelined: Google walkout organizers say company retaliated. *The Guardian*.

9   Burgess, K. (4 Mar. 2019). Ted Baker founder quits amid allegations. *The Times*.

10   Dalton, J. (3 Dec. 2018). Ted Baker staff demand end of 'forced hugging and culture of harassment'. *Independent*.

11   Keen, J. (6 Sep. 2010). Don Draper on compensation [video]. *YouTube*. https://www.youtube.com/watch?v=w2MV-x924KA.

12   Gallup (2017). State of the American workplace. https://www.gallup.com/workplace/238085/state-american-workplace-report-2017.aspx.

13   Usborne, D. (20 Jan. 2012). The moment it all went wrong for Kodak. *Independent*.

14   Maloney, J. (9 May 2017). Coke's new CEO James Quincey to staff: Make mistakes. *The Wall Street Journal*.

15   Kirsch, N. (19 Jul. 2018). The inside story of Papa John's toxic culture. *Forbes*.

16   Zarya, V. (21 May 2018). The share of female CEOs in the Fortune 500 dropped by 25% in 2018. *Fortune*.

17   Krivkovich, A., Nadeau, M.-C., Robinson, K., Robinson, N., Starikova, I. and Yee, L. (Oct. 2018). Women in the workplace. McKinsey & Co. https://www.mckinsey.com/featured-insights/gender-equality/women-in-the-workplace-2018.

18   Kollewe, J. (17 Jul. 2018). Number of women in top boardroom positions fall, says report. *The Guardian*.

19   Cox, J. (8 Mar. 2018). More people called David and Steve lead FTSE 100 Companies than women and ethnic minorities. *Independent*.

20 Sandberg, S. (27 Sep. 2016). Women are leaning in – but they face pushback. *The Wall Street Journal*.

21 Christensen, A. (5 Oct. 2017). Delivering bad news? Don't beat around the bush. Brigham Young University.

2 Culture

1 American Heart Association. Ethics policy details. https://www. heart.org/en/about-us/statements-and-policies/american-heart-association-ethics-policy-details.

2 The Chronicle of Philanthropy. Employer Profile: World Wildlife Fund (WWF). https://www.philanthropy.com/page/Employer-Profile-World/591.

3 Coca-Cola Journey. Mission, vision and values. https://www. coca-cola.co.uk/about-us/mission-vision-and-values.

4 Marriott International. Core values & heritage. https://www. marriott.com/culture-and-values/core-values.mi.

5 Google. Ten things we know to be true. https://www.google.com/ about/philosophy.html.

6 Whole Foods Market. Our core values. https://www. wholefoodsmarket.com/mission-values/core-values.

7 Facebook Careers. Facebook's 5 core values. https://www. facebook.com/pg/facebookcareers/photos/?tab=album&album_ id=1655178611435493.

8 Bryant, A. (9 Jan. 2010). On a scale of 1 to 10, how weird are you? *New York Times*.

9 Barsade, S. G. and O'Neill, O. A. (2014). What's love got to do with it? A longitudinal study of the culture of companionate love and employee and client outcomes in a long-term care setting. *Administrative Science Quarterly*, 59 (4), 551–98.

10 Bernstein, E., Shore, J. and Lazer, D. (2018). How intermittent

breaks in interaction improve collective intelligence. *Proceedings of the National Academy of Sciences*, 115 (35), 8734–9.

11 Duhigg, C. (25 Feb. 2016). What Google learned from its quest to build the perfect team. *New York Times*.

12 Wiseman, L., McKeown, G. and Covey, S. R. (2010). *Multipliers: How the Best Leaders Make Everyone Smarter*. HarperBusiness.

13 Cross, R., Rebele, R. and Grant, A. (2016). Collaborative overload. *Harvard Business Review*, 94 (1), 16.

14 Netflix. Netflix culture. https://jobs.netflix.com/culture.

15 Sainato, M. (10 Sep. 2018). Tesla workers speak out: 'Anything pro-union is shut down really fast'. *The Guardian*.

3 Communication

1 Wikiquote (30 Nov. 2018). Diana, Princess of Wales. https://en.wikiquote.org/wiki/Diana,_Princess_of_Wales.

2 Isaacson, W. (2011). *Steve Jobs*. Simon & Schuster.

3 Trump, D. and Schwartz, T. (1987). *Trump: The Art of the Deal*. Random House.

4 Robinson, J. (28 Apr. 2017). 'It's worse than a refugee camp'. *Daily Mail*.

5 Kellaway, L. (16 Jul. 2017). How I lost my 25-year battle against corporate claptrap. *Financial Times*.

4 Service

1 Hammond, D. (17 Feb. 2019). Flybmi: Passengers stranded in Europe as firm advertised flights in final hours before administration. *Telegraph*.

2 Young, R. (26 Apr. 2019). Failed airline FlyBMI 'owed £37m' when it collapsed, say administrators. *BBC News*.

3   Colson, T. (15 Feb. 2017). Bad customer service cost UK companies over £37 billion a year. *Business Insider*.

4   Hsieh, T. (2010). *Delivering Happiness: A path to profits, passion, and purpose*. Grand Central Publishing.

5   Giacobbe, A. (15 Aug. 2017). How Glossier hacked social media to build a cult-like following. *Entrepreneur*.

6   Solomon, M. (21 Apr. 2015). Ritz-Carlton president Herve Humler's leadership, culture and customer service secrets. *Forbes*.

7   Zak, P. (2017). *Trust Factor: The science of creating high-performance companies*. Amazon.

5 Money

1   Walters, J. (22 Sep. 2015). Marin Shkreli: Entrepreneur defends decision to raise price of life-saving drugs 50-fold. *The Guardian*.

2   Rushe, D. and Glenza, J. (9 Mar. 2018). Martin Shkreli jailed: 'Pharma Bro' sentenced to seven years for fraud. *The Guardian*.

3   CSR Wire (17 Dec. 2000). Enron named #22 of '100 best companies to work for in America'. https://www.csrwire.com/press_releases/25879-Enron-Named-22-Of-8220-100-Best-Companies-To-Work-For-In-America-8221-; The Street (23 Apr. 2012). Enron 10 years after – from bad to worse. *Forbes*.

4   Tran, M. and Khaw, S. (6 Jul. 2006). Enron. *The Guardian*.

5   Associated Press in New York (28 Dec. 2018). Wells Fargo to pay $575m settlement for setting up fake banking accounts. *The Guardian*.

6   Price, M. (2016). *Fairness for All: Unlocking the power of employee engagement*. David Fickling Books.

7   Smith, R. (25 Oct. 2018). Gender pay gap in the UK: 2018. Office for National Statistics. https://www.ons.gov.uk/employmentandlabourmarket/peopleinwork/earningsandworkinghours/bulletins/genderpaygapintheuk/2018.

8   Butler, S. (5 Apr. 2018). The UK companies reporting the biggest gender pay gaps. *The Guardian*.

9   Cowley, S. (23 Jul. 2018). Nike will raise wage for thousands after outcry over inequality. *New York Times*.

10 Gabbatt, A. (27 Apr. 2019). Disney heir on CEO's $66m pay: 'No one on the freaking planet is worth that'. *The Guardian*.

11 Rushe, D. (16 Aug. 2018). US bosses now earn 312 times the average worker's wage, figures show. *The Guardian*.

12 Chambers, G. and Herbert, T. (6 Jun. 2019). Jeff Bezos net worth 2019: Is the Amazon CEO still the richest person in the world after divorcing wife MacKenzie? How much is his new house worth? *Evening Standard*.

13 Jacobs, S. (11 Jan. 2018). Meet the nine richest people in the world, who have a combined fortune of $674 billion. *Independent*.

14 CIPD in association with High Pay Centre (Aug. 2018). Executive pay: Review of FTSE 100 executive pay. http://highpaycentre.org/files/CEO_pay_report.pdf.

15 Neate, R. (21 Dec. 2018). Ex-Persimmon chief fails to set up charity after anger over £75m bonus. *The Guardian*.

6 Recruitment

1   Yancey-Bragg, N. (29 Apr. 2019). Company apologizes for job posting seeking 'preferably Caucasian' candidate. *USA Today*.

2   Paul, K. (30 Apr. 2019). Tech firm apologizes after job ad seeks 'preferably Caucasian' candidates. *The Guardian*.

3   Social Mobility & Child Poverty Commission (Jun. 2015). A qualitative evaluation of non-educational barriers to the elite professions. https://assets.publishing.service.gov.uk/government/uploads/system/uploads/attachment_data/file/434791/A_

qualitative_evaluation_of_non-educational_barriers_to_the_elite_professions.pdf.

4   Scheiber, N. and Isaac, M. (19 Mar. 2019). Facebook halts ads targeting cited in bias complaints. *New York Times*.

5   Zillman, C. (24 Aug. 2015). Target to pay $2.8 million for discriminatory hiring tests. *Fortune*.

6   Cox, J. (18 Jul. 2017). Black, Asian and minority ethnic groups still grossly underrepresented in UK management, study finds. *Independent*.

7   British Academy of Management/Chartered Management Institute (Jul. 2017). Delivering diversity. Race and ethnicity in the management pipeline. https://www.managers.org.uk/~/media/Files/PDF/Insights/CMI_BAM_Delivering_Diversity_2017_Executive_Summary_Website_Copy.pdf.

8   Green Park. Leadership 10,000 (2018). https://www.green-park.co.uk/insights/leadership-10-000-2018/.

9   McKinsey & Company (Jan. 2018). Delivering through diversity. https://www.mckinsey.com/~/media/mckinsey/business%20functions/organization/our%20insights/delivering%20through%20diversity/delivering-through-diversity_full-report.ashx.

10 Cavendish, C. (28 Apr. 2019). Forget acting your age: The new rules of being Young-Old. *Telegraph*.

7 Start-Ups

1   Carreyrou, J. (16 Oct. 2015). Hot startup Theranos has struggled with its blood-test technology. *The Wall Street Journal*.

2   Carreyrou, J. (2018). *Bad Blood: Secrets and lies in a Silicon Valley startup*. Knopf.

3   Nilsson, P. (12 Oct. 2017). London start-ups are most likely to fail. *Financial Times*.

4   Burn-Callander, R. (15 Sep. 2015). 'Incompetent' bosses behind start-up failures. *Telegraph*.

5   Dann, K. (20 Jun. 2014). In the spotlight... Jo Fairley from Green & Black's. *The Guardian*.

6   CB Insights (2 Feb. 2018). The top 20 reasons startups fail. https://www.cbinsights.com/research/startup-failure-reasons-top/.

8 Crisis Management

1   Wong, J. C. (22 Nov. 2018). Facebook policy chief admits hiring PR firm to attack George Soros. *The Guardian*.

2   Dwoskin, E. (11 Mar. 2010). Zuckerberg says he's going all in on private messaging. Facebook's declining user numbers tell us why. *The Washington Post*.

3   Eleftheriou-Smith, L.-M. (19 Apr. 2017). Adidas apologizes for marketing email congratulating people for 'surviving' Boston Marathon. *Independent*.

4   Ritschel, C. (26 Mar. 2019). Krispy Kreme owners plan to donate £8.3m over Nazi family ties. *Independent*.

5   Wattles, J. (13 Apr. 2017). Digging itself out of a hole: How United's PR response evolved. *CNN Business*.

6   Press Association (8 Jan. 2018). H&M apologises over image of black child in 'monkey' hoodie. *The Guardian*.

7   Zhang, M. M. (24 Nov. 2018). Dolce & Gabbana cancelled chopsticks advert shows us orientalism is finally being taken seriously as a form of racism. *Independent*.

8   Hosie, R. (30 May 2018). What Starbucks employees learned on their racial bias training day. *Independent*.

9 Responsibility

1   3p Contributor (28 Oct. 2015). CSR after Volkswagen scandal. *Triple Pundit.* https://www.triplepundit.com/story/2015/csr-after-volkswagen-scandal/30846; Volkswagen. Compliance & risk management. https://www.volkswagenag.com/en/group/compliance-and-risk-management.html.

2   Chapman, B. (15 Apr. 2019). German prosecutors charge former Volkswagen boss Martin Winterkorn with fraud. *Independent.*

3   [No author] (12 Sep. 2017). Bell Pottinger collapses after South African scandal. *BBC News.*

4   Chouinard, Y. (2006). *Let My People Go Surfing: The education of a reluctant businessman.* Penguin.

5   [No author] (29 Nov. 2018). Patagonia's $10 million donation: Why they give away their US tax savings. *BBC News.*

6   Somerville, H. (19 Apr. 2018). Lyft to offset emissions from rides with projects combating climate change. Reuters UK.

7   Cone. 2015 Cone Communications/Ebiquity Global CSR Study. http://www.conecomm.com/research-blog/2015-cone-communications-ebiquity-global-csr-study.

8   Topham, G. (26 Jun. 2018). Uber wins 15-month probationary licence to work in London. *The Guardian.*

9   [No author] (22 Aug. 2018). Uber to pay $1.9m for sexual harassment claims. *BBC News.*

10 [No author] (11 Jul. 2018). Uber executive resigns after race discrimination probe. *BBC News.*

11 Bosa, D. (14 May 2018). Lyft claims it now has more than one-third of the US ride-sharing market. *CNBC News.*

12 Isaac, M., de la Merced, M. J. and Sorkin, A. R. (15 May 2019). How the promise of a $120 billion Uber I.P.O. evaporated. *New York Times.*

13 Burkus, D. (2 Jul. 2015). The real reason Google serves all that free food. *Forbes.*

14 Kadakia, C. (1 Mar. 2016). How one man began a culture of good that reduced turnover at retailer, TCC. *Hackernoon.*

15 Strom, S. (26 Jun. 2016). Perdue aims to make chickens happier and more comfortable. *New York Times.*

16 Yuan, M. (30 Apr. 2015). Fur trading shows no signs of slowing down in Asia. *Forbes.*

Conclusion – Success

1 The Body Shop (24 Oct. 2018). *Facebook.* https://www.facebook.com/TheBodyShopPakistan/photos/a.129104777190632/1542442969190132/?type=1&theater.

Acknowledgements

A few years ago I found myself completely naked in probably one of the most incredible saunas in the world, as a guest of Maria Hauser at Stanglwirt Hotel in Kitzbuhel, Austria. I sat naked in my slightly prudish, English way next to American author, journalist and great thinker Val Frankel. Val had just heard me speak at the Global Wellness Summit and asked me if I'd ever written a book about the business values, ethics and philosophies that I'd been talking about. The rest is history. Without Val this book would not exist and I am deeply indebted to her.

I'd also like to thank my fabulous literary agents, Dan Strone and Dorothy Vincent of Trident Media Group, for taking me on, and of course Mike Harpley at Atlantic Books for believing in this book and publishing it.

Life does not often offer up a chance meeting that changes your life. Tom Konig-Oppenheimer – you are an extraordinary human being and I have been deeply blessed to have shared nineteen years with you. Quite literally, you changed my life. Daniel Marks – you are what my father would call, quite simply, *'una persona buona'*. A good, decent, honest person. As we say in the industry, 'without you I am nothing' and, joking apart, it is true. Without the two of you... And John Frieda, thank you. You taught me so, so much, challenged me, made me think and learn. I hope some of the things you taught me are in this book for others to learn from. I could not be more grateful for all you have given me.

Thank you also to everyone who is and is not mentioned in this book. Every client of The Communications Store, every member of staff who is not mentioned by name, every editor, journalist, writer and supporter of our company who has helped us, believed in us and given us incredible opportunities.

And thank you always to my beautiful husband Mungo, who supports me, listens to me, guides me and grounds me. How very lucky I am.

And, finally, a thank you to my beloved daughters, Valentina and Darcy. May this book and my love help you to navigate a complicated world and give you the strength to know, deep down, what is right. And follow through. Walk the talk, don't talk the talk. Thank you also for inspiring me, as your Mamma, to try to show you the way. You can, you can, you can. If you want to.

Index